PROJECT LEADERSHIP

For other McGraw-Hill titles by James P. Lewis:

Mastering Project Management: Applying Advanced Concepts of Systems Thinking, Control and Evaluation, and Resource Allocation

Project Planning Schedule & Control: A Hands-On Guide to Bringing Projects in on Time and on Budget
Third Edition

The Project Manager's Desk Reference
Second Edition

Working Together: 12 Principles for Achieving Excellence in Managing Projects, Teams, and Organizations

PROJECT LEADERSHIP

James P. Lewis

Boston, Massachusetts   Burr Ridge, Illinois
Dubuque, Iowa   Madison, Wisconsin   New York, New York
San Francisco, California   St. Louis, Missouri

Copyright © 2003 by James P. Lewis. All rights reserved. Printed in the United States of America. Except as permitted under the United States Copyright Act of 1976, no part of this publication may be reproduced, stored in a retrieval system, or transmitted, in any form or by any means, electronic, mechanical, photocopying, recording, or otherwise, without the prior written permission of the publisher.

2 3 4 5 6 7 8 9   BKM BKM   0 9 8 7 6 5

ISBN 0-07-138867-2

McGraw-Hill books are available at special quantity discounts to use as premiums and sales promotions, or for use in corporate training programs. For more information, please write to the Director of Special Sales, McGraw-Hill, Professional Publishing, 2 Penn Plaza, New York, NY 10121-2298. Or contact your local bookstore.

This publication is designed to provide accurate and authoritative information in regard to the subject matter covered. It is sold with the understanding that neither the author nor the publisher is engaged in rendering legal, accounting, or other professional service. If legal advice or other expert assistance is required, the services of a competent professional should be sought.
—*From a Declaration of Principles jointly adopted by a Committee of the American Bar Association and a Committee of Publishers.*

Library of Congress Cataloging-in-Publication Data

Lewis, James P., 1941–
    Project leadership / by James P. Lewis.
      p. cm.
    ISBN 0-07-138867-2 (pbk.)
    1. Leadership.   2. Project management.   I. Title.
HD57.7 .L476 2002
658.4′04—dc21

                                                    2002011497

This book is dedicated to

Julian S. Stubbs

Who is more a leader than a manager

Those who
say it
cannot be done

should not

interrupt
the person
doing it.
~
Chinese proverb

Great Wall of China
photo by Jim Lewis - trip to China 2002

Contents

Preface

*W*arren Bennis, who has enjoyed an outstanding career for nearly 50 years as a student and writer on leadership, has said that "We have too many managers and not enough leaders" (Bennis, 2000). How right he is. I have been teaching project management for over 20 years, and most of my students have been interested primarily in the *tools* of project management—work breakdown structures, critical path scheduling, and earned value analysis. Few of them have been concerned with leadership.

In fact, I received an evaluation from one individual who commented that "Most of the seminar was okay, except for the 30 percent on *touchy-feely* stuff." What he doesn't understand, and I am sure this is true of many of my students, is that without the ability to deal effectively with people, the tools of project management may be of little more use than to help him document his failures with great precision.

I have commented in many of my books that project managers often have a lot of responsibility and very little authority, because they have team members who report to functional managers.

When I made this comment in China recently, I was asked, "Dr. Lewis, if he has no authority, how does he get anything done?"

Unfortunately, I am not always quick on my feet, and it was only after I returned from China that I thought of a good response. I should have asked, "Why are you in the audience? Did someone force you to come here?" I know the answer. They came of their own accord. Why? Because they wanted to get something from my lecture.

In other words, they were influenced to attend because of WIIFM—What's In It For Me? And this is one of the most important things for a leader to understand—that people perform tasks because there is some payback involved. Failing to recognize that followers must receive rewards for their involvement leads to managing, rather than leading.

The problem is that there are two kinds of authority—that in which I can tell people what to do and expect them to do it, and there is authority to make decisions without getting approval from a higher authority. The first kind of authority is the one that few project managers have, but the second one we need more of.

However, it should be noted that even if you have authority over people, it does not guarantee that they will do what you tell them. Many CEOs have told me that the only thing authority gives them is the right to exercise sanctions over people who do not do what they are told. Authority does not, however, guarantee compliance, because people work in an organization by choice—if they become discontent, they will leave. (This is not so true in Asian countries, but there are other social forces at work that do not apply in the United States, so it is very difficult to make general statements that are true cross-culturally.)

In any case, it is important to realize that only by exercising leadership can a project manager expect to be optimally successful. The good news is that leadership can be learned, and that is why I have written this book. Certainly we may not all be equally effective at the discipline, but we can "level the playing field" through determination and practice.

There are many good books on leadership. I have tried to add some dimensions to this one that the others do not contain, and especially the dimension of leading project teams, which is different than managing teams in general.

I hope you find it useful, and welcome your comments and suggestions. You can reach me at the e-mail address listed below.

James P. Lewis
Vinton, Virginia
July 2002
jlewis@lewisinstitute.com

Acknowledgments

I want to thank my editor, Catherine Dassopoulos, for her enthusiastic support for this and all of my book projects. I have lost count of how many projects I have done with Catherine, but it has always been a pleasure to work with her.

As usual, my wife, Lea Ann, has put her soul into making the book look like more than dull, printed words. Readers consistently tell me how much they like the art in my books, and the credit all goes to her.

Since Lea Ann is not proficient at the computer, we owe special thanks to Lora Hansen for implementing the concepts on the computer.

Judy Brown has now typeset a number of my books, and she does such a good job that I always ask for her to be assigned to my projects. As usual, she has done an excellent job on this book.

There are many people who have contributed to my thinking on leadership. One of the most influential has been Alan Mulally, president and CEO of Boeing Commercial Airplanes. His *Working Together* principles have been very helpful to me in clarifying my outlook on leadership, and are discussed more fully in my book by that name. I can't claim to know too many CEOs of large companies, but of those I have known, Alan is one who can truly be called a leader.

1

What Is Leadership? And Do We Really Need It?

*W*hy are you reading this? What prompted you to pick up this book in the first place? Was it the catchy title or the attractive book jacket? Or did your boss or your spouse hand it to you and say, "You need help—read this!"

Presumably, no matter how the book came into your hands, you feel the need to be a leader. But why? Where do you want to take people that is so important? And why should anyone want to follow your lead in the first place? These are the first two questions that you must answer before you can hope to be a leader.

By definition, a leader gets people to follow him or her to some destination. It goes without saying that if no one is following you, then you aren't a leader. So if you are reading this book, it must mean that you want to have followers—people who will go along

FOLLOWERS & LEADERS

If no one is following you, then you aren't a leader.

with you to wherever you're going and help you achieve whatever you want to achieve.

NAME SOME LEADERS

Before going any further, write down a list of all the leaders you can think of. They can be political, religious, or business leaders, or leaders of social clubs or societies you belong to. List people who inspire others to follow them willingly. Stop reading now and take a few moments to make a list.

* * * * *

Now, did your list contain people like Gandhi, Churchill, John F. Kennedy, Yasser Arafat, Adolph Hitler, Mayor Rudolph Giuliani, President George Bush? If not, would you add them to your list? If not, why not?

Consider Hitler, for example. Hitler was a leader. He was. But many people will not put his name on their list, because what he stood for horrifies them. It horrifies me as well. But I can't escape the fact that a large number of people followed him willingly.

Were there any members of street gangs on your list? They are leaders, you know. They have willing followers.

How about Osama bin Laden? Again, a despicable leader, but a leader nevertheless.

The point is that you can't call people leaders only when they stand for something good and reject those who stand for something bad. If they are able to gain willing followers, they are leaders, like it or not. We just don't want to be like the ones who stand for bad things.

LEADING VERSUS MANAGING

Vance Packard has captured the essence of leadership in the definition shown in the box. Note that the most important word in his definition is *want*. A leader gets others to *want* to do something that he wants them to do. A person may be able to *coerce* others to do something—people with guns do this. But such behavior is not leadership. Furthermore, managers (and parents) sometimes

> *Leadership appears to be the art of getting others to want to do something that you are convinced should be done.*
> — Vance Packard

induce people to do things they don't really want to do by offering big rewards. This leads to compliance, but there is a significant difference between compliance and commitment. Leaders are able to gain commitment from people.

Followers who act out of commitment don't have to be watched all the time to ensure that they give the activity their best effort. People who are only complying with directives may have to be watched because they quit working every time the boss turns her back. It should be clear that a project manager—especially—has to gain commitment from team members because one of the facts of life for project managers is that they have a lot of responsibility and very little authority. So they must get team members to commit to the project, or they will have a difficult time getting the level of performance needed to achieve project objectives.

> *Followers who act out of commitment don't have to be watched all the time to ensure their best effort.*

Warren Bennis, a student of leadership for over 50 years, has observed that we have too many managers and not enough leaders (2000). To understand why he says this, we should consider the meaning of the word *manage*. To manage originally meant to handle horses. It comes from the French. The word evolved to mean to handle the scheduling, budgeting, and other administrative aspects of a job.

Dr. Peter Drucker is generally credited with having established management as a profession. At one time, owners of businesses ran everything. Of course, as an organization grew, no one individual could oversee everything, so intermediaries had to be appointed to coordinate some of the jobs that needed doing. These people were initially thought of in a way similar to that of the military. There is the commanding officer, who other officers of lower rank report to, and on down the hierarchy they go until you reach the troops at the bottom of the ladder. This *command-and-control* way of thinking has dominated organizations for a long time.

However, even the military realized some time ago that compliance with orders was insufficient—that they too needed to gain commitment from the troops, and they have invested heavily in leadership training for their officers. Unfortunately, U. S. organizations by and large don't seem to have realized the need for leadership. We have MBA programs at most major universities turning out managers, but very few of these programs are developing leaders. And when an organization does realize that its managers are not leading people, they try to teach them leadership in short seminars that seldom do more than make trainees aware of their deficiencies.

Unfortunately, the difference between managing and leading has become blurred by our careless use of language. People who are in official positions of management are not necessarily leaders but are often referred to as such. Some managers have people reporting to them who do what they are told like uninspired drones, and these managers bitterly complain about how unresponsive and unmotivated their people are. They generally look for a way of "fixing" the workers who report to them, rather than asking what needs to be corrected in their own behavior. To repeat my earlier question, these managers should ask themselves, "Why would anyone want to follow my lead?"

I believe this question really amounts to asking what motivates people, and the answer to that question is that people are motivated to satisfy their needs. It's as simple as that, and as complex as understanding that needs differ, so that "one-size-fits-all" does not work when it comes to motivating people. Yes, there are categories of needs, but how each individual satisfies those needs is specific to that person. So if you want to entice people with cheese, you need to know what kind of cheese he or she finds appetizing.

The general categories of needs that all human beings have are physiological (biological), security or safety, social, esteem or recognition, and self-actualization. These names were used by Abraham Maslow to describe the categories of needs that we have, and were arranged in a hierarchy with physiological needs at the bottom and self-actualization at the top. The term *self-actualization* was a term coined by Maslow to mean that a person wants to fully express and develop him- or herself—to be, as Maslow said, everything that he or she can be.

The hierarchy was based on the belief that if a person has basic biological (physiological) needs that are unmet, she won't be much

What motivates people?

———

People are motivated to satisfy their needs.

interested in social or esteem needs. As these lower level needs are met, however, the higher level needs become more active. Extensive research has generally failed to validate the idea of a hierarchy, so I caution against accepting it as reliable. In fact, I believe that the opposite might even be argued—that is, when a person is self-actualizing, the other needs become less important. So I believe that, to achieve real motivation in the organization, we should make it possible for people to self-actualize, and the other needs will be more easily satisfied. We will revisit this issue later on.

For now, I think it is sufficient to understand that if you want people to willingly follow your lead, you must ensure that their needs will be met in doing so. The old principle, what's in it for me? (WIIFM), is a reliable guide to leadership. I believe you will find that it is being practiced by any individual who is a true leader.

LEADERSHIP IS NOT A POSITION

As I said earlier, many people are *officially* leaders by virtue of their position in the organization but are not really leaders. In terms of power, we say that they have position power or legitimate power, but that is quite different from leadership. In other words, people may comply with their directives, but without *wanting* to do so. This is, again, the crucial test.

What this means is that leadership is granted by followers. We will see later on that it is an exchange relationship, in which followers confer to the leader the right to lead the way while they follow, but this contract will be revoked if the leader fails to deliver on his or her part of the bargain.

James McGregor Burns may have been the first author to make a strong case for the fact that studying leadership as a unilateral thing is not very helpful. We must understand the nature of "followership" if we are to understand leadership, and there has been significantly less research done in this area than on leadership itself.

Therefore, to truly understand leadership—and to be a leader—we must take followership very seriously; and we must understand the nature of the people we want to follow us, or we cannot hope to be successful.

WHEN IS LEADERSHIP NEEDED?

There seems to be a belief that all managers need to be leaders all of the time. I have even thought this myself, until I started to write this book. Throughout my graduate program in psychology, I studied leadership, teams, and organizational behavior. I was a project manager when I started my program, then I became a department manager. And I wanted to know how to get people to do what needed doing with more motivation, enthusiasm, and commitment. So the topic of leadership had immediate relevance for my job.

As I started working on this book, I began to examine my beliefs. I began to question when leadership is really needed, and I was surprised at what I realized. First, it is not important that leadership be exercised all the time! There are some jobs that are routine, operations-oriented, that don't seem to require leadership. Here is an example.

In the early part of my new career as a seminar instructor, before I began teaching project management full time, I taught a number of courses on managing. One of these was entitled, *How to Reduce Absenteeism and Turnover*. At the time I lived in North Carolina, and most of my programs were conducted there and in surrounding states. The first question I asked on beginning this program was, "Tell me what levels of absenteeism and turnover you have in your organizations." Absenteeism figures usually ranged from a few percent to around 10 percent maximum. Turnover was another story.

"Our turnover is 10 percent," said one person, with a twinge of delight in how bad it was (perhaps playing the game of "ain't it awful"). "That's nothing," said another participant. "Ours is 60 percent!"

Gasps of disbelief echoed off the walls, and people asked, "Where in the world do you work?"

"The poultry processing plant," said the winner of round one of the ain't it awful contest. But he was soon upstaged.

"I wish ours was that low," barked another contestant. "Ours is 250 percent!" He sat back and gloated at having totally demolished the previous contestant, while other participants commiserated and realized how lucky they were with only 10 or 12 percent.

Of course, the winner also worked for a poultry processing plant. So I asked the standard question of the winner and runner-up. "Do you take job applicants out into the plant and let them see for themselves the nature of the job, so that they know it is not a nice clean office job?"

They assured me that they did. However, they explained that most of their applicants were desperate for work, and no doubt convinced themselves that they could stomach the job of gutting chickens, but after being hired they continued with their job search, and as soon as something more desirable came along, they were gone. So the next question I asked was, "Do you have people in the job who have been with you several years and seem fairly content with the job?"

The answer was yes.

"Then you need to find out what characteristics these people have in common," I advised, "and use that profile to screen new

Poor fit = Poor performance

If you hire people into a job who aren't suited for it, you can expect degraded performance and possible turnover.

$E=mc^2$

applicants. If you can hire people with similar characteristics, then you can expect them to stay with you longer than those who don't fit the profile." This is a fairly standard approach to the problem of reducing turnover. If you hire people into a job who aren't suited for it, then you can expect degraded performance and possible turnover as a result.

Now back to the question of leadership, which is the art of getting people to *want* to do something. I have strong doubts that there are people in this world who want to kill and clean chickens for a living. Rather, I believe that the people who do these jobs over long periods of time are either resigned to this livelihood as the best they can do, or perhaps on a positive note, they take pride in doing something that most other people couldn't stomach doing. So there may not be a lot of motivation involved. There may be commitment to do a good job, but not a lot of drive in the process. I will admit that I am speculating, as I know of no studies that have been done to prove me right. Still, if I am right, not much leadership is needed in such a situation. The job is routine, repetitive, and requires only that each person on the line work at the proper pace, so the line doesn't stall. Management skills may be required of supervisors, but that is all.

9

I believe that this is true of many operations kind of jobs. Those that are fairly rote and repetitive do not require a lot of drive on the part of the people doing them. I believe that these jobs fit what Frederick Herzberg called "maintenance factors." So long as working conditions are acceptable, the work doesn't provide much in the way of motivation. If conditions become unacceptable, however, the job becomes a demotivator, and the person will either slack off or leave the job.

Conditions that Require Leadership

Peter Drucker once wrote that the job of a manager is to get workers to go beyond the minimum acceptable level of performance in their jobs (1973). Drucker's argument was that minimum-acceptable performance only ensures that an organization can survive. However, it cannot excel, and therefore it is unlikely to be a very strong force in the marketplace.

Now, while I believe that there are jobs that are so mundane and even distasteful that it is nearly impossible to get people excited about doing them, there are others where it is possible to motivate workers to go beyond minimum requirements, and I believe that it is here that leadership is needed. We have found, for example, that people in self-directed work teams can be truly motivated by their work. This is primarily because the job has been enriched and enlarged, offering workers a chance to grow and develop their skills. In these working arrangements, the role of the supervisor changes from that of command-and-control to that of facilitator, which to me means that leadership is actually the *modus operandi*, rather than managing.

I have interviewed a number of leaders of self-directed work teams, and they have all told me that there is no such thing as a leaderless team. However, they emphasize that leadership is shared. At any given time, the requirements of the task will dictate who emerges as leader of the team.

What this means is that to understand leadership, you must understand that there is an interaction between the task, the follower, and the leader. This is shown in Figure 1.1. At the intersection of the three circles you have effective performance of the team.

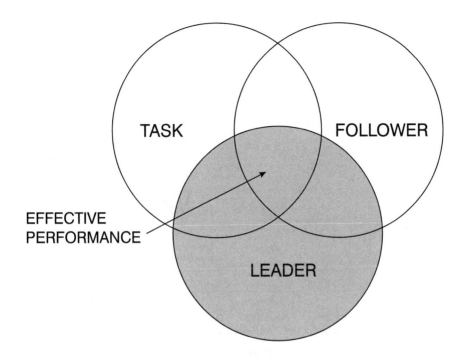

Figure 1.1
Venn diagram showing task, follower, leader.

Project Leadership

I think it can be argued that all projects require that team members go beyond minimally acceptable performance because projects are always one-time jobs, rather than repetitive, mundane, rote work. Because each project addresses a need that must be met for the organization to thrive in a competitive environment, it is hard for me to imagine a project in which leadership is not required.

Now, since leadership is essentially an interaction with people, I have long held the position that the most important skills a project manager must have are "people skills." I have shown this using the model of project management systems shown in Figure 1.2.

I have placed human relations skills at the bottom of the pyramid because it is the base of the structure, and if the foundation of a structure is weak, the entire thing may collapse. So in my

11

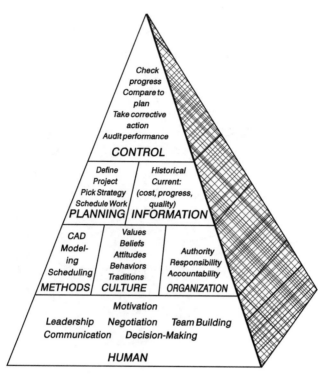

Figure 1.2
Lewis model of systems.

seminars I state very firmly that these skills are essential in order to make everything above work correctly. When my class is mostly comprised of technologists, I sometimes get moans and groans from participants, who say, "I really hate that stuff." To which I reply that they should reconsider their careers. If they hate dealing with "people problems," they will tend to avoid them, and the problems will escalate until an explosion occurs and disrupts the project.

I even had one programmer complain that he saw no need for establishing rapport with team members. "After all," he said, "we're technical people. We deal with logic and problem solving. What good is all that touchy-feely stuff?"

I suggested that we test it. I said, "Imagine that I'm the team leader, and I come to your desk and say, 'John, we've got a problem. We need to talk.'" He thought that was okay. Then I said, "Suppose instead, I simply do it this way. I approach you and say,

'Hi John. You have a minute? I need to talk with you about a problem.' Which do you prefer?"

He admitted that he preferred the more "polite" approach. Why? Because it conveys respect for the individual. It doesn't take for granted that he has time to talk with me just now. And it paves the way for a more cooperative interaction with him than I might get with the "direct" approach.

The problem is that in many organizations, we place people in leadership positions because of their technical excellence (which often equates with poor social skills), and wonder why their teams don't perform very well. There are many exceptions to what I'm saying, of course. You find teams led by technical experts that hum like well-oiled machines. It is usually because the members of the team have so much respect for the technical skills of the leader that they work well together. But even then, you often find that the real leader may not be the official person, but some other member of the team who translates the technical expert's desires into terms that the team can understand and get excited about.

Now I said that I suggest that individuals who hate dealing with "people issues" not be project managers. However, there are many technical experts who say, "I don't mind dealing with these things, but I'm not very good at it." I suggest that they simply put together a self-development plan to gain interpersonal skills. It can all be learned—if you want to. So if you are one of those individuals who is interested in becoming a leader, continue reading. You can do it.

If you're someone who hates dealing with people, sell this book to someone else. It isn't for you.

2

Leadership in Action—Some Examples

Leadership is, above all else, an *influence* process. A leader is able to get people to want to do things he or she wants done. That being the case, we need to examine influence processes, and one way to do that is to look at examples of real leadership in action.

A leadership process that is accessible to everyone is that of Jaime Escalante. He was born in La Paz, Bolivia, where he taught physics and math for 14 years. In 1964, he moved to the United States, by way of the University of Puerto Rico, then on to California. He then studied nights at the Pasadena City College to learn English and obtain a degree in electronics.

In 1976, he began teaching at Garfield High School, in east Los Angeles, where drugs, gangs, and violence were facts of daily life. Despite all this, Escalante was able to motivate 18 students to take and pass the AP calculus exam in 1982. By 1991, the number of

> *Leadership is above all else, an INFLUENCE process.*

Garfield students taking the advanced placement examinations in math and other subjects had increased to 570. That was the year Escalante left the school, citing faculty politics and petty jealousies. He was hired by the Sacramento school system almost instantly.

He is considered one of the most famous educators in the United States. He was the subject of the 1988 movie *Stand and Deliver*, which dramatized his efforts to help underachieving Latino students beat the odds and pass the AP calculus test. This semi-documentary about Escalante (played by Edward James Olmos) has become one of the classic films about American education. In recognition of his achievements, Escalante was awarded the United States Presidential Medal and the Andres Bello award by the Organization of American States (www.boliviaweb.com/hallfame/escalante.htm).

ESCALANTE'S METHODS

The best way to grasp the power of Escalante's leadership approach is to watch the movie, *Stand and Deliver*, which is available for rent in many video rental stores in the United States. In the first class

T-E-A-M-S

Leadership is getting people to want to do something, which means giving them motivation for doing it.

scene, Escalante enters a room in mild chaos. Students are milling around, rough-housing with each other, and are generally uninterested in being in a math class. Many of them are Latino; all of them have very little competence in math. In fact, Escalante was initially supposed to teach them fractions—basic math.

He begins by doing some very unorthodox things. One of the students wears a net over his hair, and he and his brother are members of a local gang. Escalante gets in his face and says, "You're on my turf now. You get out of line, and you're in trouble." He addresses the student as "nethead."

Now the first thing you may think is that this is very disrespectful. Maybe. However, it is a fact that you can only deal effectively with someone if you have first gained his respect, and for a member of a gang, that respect must usually be gained by a show of force. So for Escalante to establish the classroom as his "turf" was something the young man could respect.

Next he turned to the class and said, "Some of you, because of your surnames and the color of your skin, have two strikes against you in this society. There are people who will think you know less than you do." He goes on to say that if the students don't do something about it, the best they can hope for in life is to work in a fast-food restaurant as "taco benders." "Math is the great equalizer," says Escalante. "If you get a good education in math, you can do anything you want to do."

What is going on? Well, remember that leadership is getting people to *want* to do something, which means giving them motivation for doing it. In this instance, Escalante is saying that they can make more of their lives by getting an education than by dropping out or just muddling through.

> *The day someone quits school, he is condemning himself to a future of poverty.*
> — Jaime Escalante

I think it is important to note here that because Escalante is Hispanic, he automatically has credibility with the students that a non-Hispanic teacher would never have had. One of the barriers to building rapport with others is any perceived difference. One of those is age difference. Another is the student-teacher contrast. So a teacher has at least two obstacles to overcome in developing a relationship with students. Had Escalante been non-Hispanic, that would have added another obstacle, one that he might never have overcome.

Next Escalante tells them, "You have math in your blood. Your ancestors, the Maya, invented the zero! All I require of you is desire—*ganas*. If you don't have the *ganas*, I'll give it to you because I am the greatest!"

In this statement, Escalante accomplishes several things at one time. First, he says math is going to be easy for these kids because their ancestors were accomplished mathematicians—a fact of considerable importance. The Maya did indeed discover the zero, something that Europeans did not do until long after the Maya, and they had also figured out the true calendar, something that also plagued Europeans for a very long time.

So Escalante is saying that this will be easy, and all they need is desire (*ganas* is the Spanish word). If they don't have the desire, he will give it to them. Now how many teachers look at it this way? Many of them bemoan that it is impossible to teach kids who don't want to learn. They use the old saw about, "You can lead a horse to water, but you can't make him drink." Escalante, on the other hand, is saying he will take responsibility for giving them the desire if they don't already have it.

How will he do that? By making a subject *relevant*, for one thing. As we have all experienced, many of the courses we were forced to take in school seemed to have no relevance in our lives (history is an example, though there may be no more relevant subject if we really taught the topic properly). So we got through them by sheer willpower, but not with enthusiasm.

Second, Escalante made the subject fun! Mercy, what heresy. Everyone knows that math is boring, dry, the furthest thing from fun that a course could possibly be. But Escalante makes it fun. How?

He is teaching simultaneous equations in one scene. If you ever took algebra, you no doubt knew students who found this part of algebra to be exceedingly difficult. But Escalante says, "Juan has two girlfriends more than Carlos. Carlos has one girlfriend less that José. How many girlfriends do they have between them?"

There is a lot of joking, as they try to work out the answer, and Escalante bemoans their stupidity at not being able to solve the puzzle—all of it good-naturedly, of course.

You may also notice that the students call him "quimo." I could never find this word in my Spanish dictionaries, but one day I met some students from South America, who told me that it is a slang term used to mean a teacher who teaches dumb kids. So these students have acknowledged that they are in need of help, and that Escalante is the teacher of a bunch of dumb kids. All of it in fun, again.

There are three other very important scenes in the movie that tell us about Escalante's leadership. One of the students is a bright girl whose father owns a restaurant. She has college potential, but her father wants her to just quit school and work in the restaurant. Escalante, with his wife, goes to the restaurant and tries to persuade the girl's father to reconsider. In the process, he is a bit less than tactful, and her father asks him to leave the restaurant. But the next day, the girl is back in class.

In another situation, one student, who is the slowest of the group, tells Escalante he is going to drop out and become an auto mechanic. He has an old Firebird that he manages to keep running through sheer determination. In one scene, Escalante is driving it, and the student is in the passenger seat. He tells Escalante that he will be a member of the union and make even more money than Escalante does. They reach a fork in the road, and Jaime asks which way he should turn. At the last moment, the student tells him which way to go, only to find that they are on a dead-end road. Escalante says, "You can see all the turns. You just can't see where they are taking you." The boy stays in the class.

Finally, after a plant tour, Escalante decides that he will teach the group calculus, so that they will get college credit for it (assuming they can pass the AP test). The head of the math department is horrified at this. She says that the students are delicate, and that if he challenges them too much, they will be set up to fail. He replies, "They will rise to the levels of our expectations for them."

This is an extremely important point. Escalante is citing the self-fulfilling prophecy, which was first validated by Rosenthal and Jacobsen (1968) in a school setting. Our followers will rise to the level of our expectations for them. For that reason, the most disrespectful thing you can do to another human being is to expect less of him or her than the person is capable of doing. When we convey to members of our project team that we expect great things of them, we tend to get great things, and vice versa.

Yes, there would be the risk of setting up these students if Escalante had simply expected great things of them and then left them to sink or swim on their own. But this is not what he did. He supported them. He encouraged them. He went to bat for them. That is true leadership!

RUDY GIULIANI, MAYOR OF THE WORLD

Although he had been mayor of New York for seven-and-three-fourths years, Rudolph (Rudy) Giuliani became a leader in the eyes of the world in the days following September 11, 2001.

Because of the way he handled the aftermath of the terrorist attacks on the World Trade Center, together with his success in reducing crime in the city, *Time* magazine named him Person of the Year (December 31, 2001–January 7, 2002). You can read the *Time* article online at www.time.com/time/poy2001/poyprofile.htm. Following is an excerpt from the article.

> *Sept. 11 was the day that Giuliani was supposed to begin the inevitable slide toward irrelevancy. It was primary-election day in the city, when people would go to the polls to begin choosing his successor. After two terms, his place in history seemed secure: great mayor, not-so-great guy. The first Republican to run the town in a generation, he had restored New York's spirit, cutting crime by two-thirds, moving 691,000 people off the welfare rolls, boosting property values and incomes in neighborhoods rich and poor, redeveloping great swaths of the city. But great swaths of the city were sick of him. People were tired of his Vesuvian temper and constant battles—against his political enemies, against some of his own appointees, against the media and city-funded museums, against black leaders and street vendors and jaywalkers and finally even against his own wife. His marriage to television personality Donna Hanover was a war: ugly headlines, dueling press conferences. Giuliani's girlfriend, a pharmaceutical-sales manager named Judith Nathan, had helped him get through a battle against prostate cancer, and his struggle touched off a wave of concern and appreciation for him. But most New Yorkers seemed ready for Rudy and Judi to leave the stage together and melt into the crowd.*
>
> *Fate had another idea. When the day of infamy came, Giuliani seized it as if he had been waiting for it all his life, taking on half a dozen critical roles and performing each masterfully. Improvising on the fly, he became America's homeland-security boss, giving calm, informative briefings about the attacks and the extraordinary response. He was the gutsy decision maker, balancing security against symbolism, overruling those who wanted to keep the city buttoned up tight, pushing key institutions—from the New York Stock Exchange to Major League Baseball—to reopen and prove that New Yorkers were getting on with life. He was the crisis manager, bringing together scores of major players from city, state and federal governments for marathon daily meetings that got*

everyone working together. And he was the consoler in chief, strong enough to let his voice brim with pain, compassion and love. When he said "the number of casualties will be more than any of us can bear," he showed a side of himself most people had never seen.

Interestingly, Giuliani drew on another one-time leader for his inspiration—Winston Churchill. He stayed up most of the night of September 11 reading the chapters on World War II from a new biography by Roy Jenkins (2001). What Churchill succeeded in doing for England during the summer of 1940 was what Giuliani did for New York. He created the illusion that they were bound to win.

Giuliani later pondered how much of what Churchill had to say was bluff. Certainly Churchill could not know for certain that England would come out of the war OK, or whether they would come under German rule. Likewise, how much of what Giuliani told the American public was bluff? As he said, "Look, in a crisis you have to be optimistic."

This is parallel with what Alan Mulally, president and CEO of Boeing Commercial Airplanes once told me. "If the leader is falling down on the floor, the team begins to think everything is falling apart," he said. "The leader has to set the context, to help people feel that they can make it." And so Rudy Giuliani did what is expected of all leaders: He helped the people find confidence in their time of crisis, confidence that the nation would survive, that the enemy would eventually pay for their crimes, and that we would go forward stronger for our pain.

ALAN MULALLY

A year before September 11, 2001, I met Alan Mulally, President and CEO of Boeing Commercial Airplanes. During that meeting, he shared his principles of management with me, and I later wrote a book entitled *Working Together* about those principles. While I was writing the book, I attended one of Alan's weekly Business Plan Review meetings, in which the entire business operation is reviewed, and I had a lot of e-mail correspondence with him. During that time, the economy was strong and Boeing was doing well. And Mulally was always upbeat, optimistic, confident in the future of Boeing.

Almost immediately after September 11, air travel dropped like a rock and airlines began canceling orders for airplanes. Boeing announced that nearly one-third of the workforce would have to be furloughed—about 37,000 people. I wondered what effect this would have on Alan. Would he maintain his optimistic outlook? I know that he is a very caring individual. How would it make him feel to have to lay off 37,000 workers?

During a visit to Boeing in February 2002, I asked a couple of high-level Boeing managers about this, and they assured me that he was as positive as ever. Then I wrote Alan and asked him for a comment on leading in a time of crisis. Here is what he wrote:

> *I think our working together principles and practices are more important than ever. . . . I have now added "people first" as the number one. We the leaders are needed more than ever to have thoughts and share our thoughts about where we think our world is going . . . our markets . . . our customers . . . our partners . . . and ourselves . . . and what do we need to do individually and as a team to deal with our current realities and create a better future for all of us going forward . . . and help each other through these tough times . . . and feel so good about this.* (Personal correspondence. Used by permission.)

Again, like Churchill, Giuliani, and Escalante, Mulally emphasizes the need to make followers feel good about themselves, to feel empowered to succeed, and to "keep one's chin up," as the expression goes.

RESEARCH FINDINGS

Psychologist David McClelland studied leadership extensively during the 1970s and found that effective leaders use different language than ineffective leaders. In particular, they talk about how *we* will succeed, how *we* will go forward, how *we* will come through a crisis. Ineffective leaders, on the other hand, use "I" language.

They talk about what *I* want to accomplish, about *my* goals, and about how *I* want to win.

The effective leader gives followers a sense of empowerment, whereas those who are not effective do the opposite—many of them actually make people feel powerless. This is, in fact, the standard style of many managers in organizations. They are *disabling*, rather than *enabling*.

I believe one reason for this is explained by the law of requisite variety. This law, which comes from systems theory, says that, in any system of humans or machines, the element with the greatest flexibility in its behavior will control the entire system. Accepting that this is true, we have some immediate implications. First, every human being eventually runs out of flexibility, and this law says that the individual's flexibility must exceed the variation presented by the system (group of people) if he or she is to be in control.

Given that we all have limits to our flexibility, the alternative is to reduce the variability in the system itself. That is, we must keep our team members from going in a million different directions since we can't match that much variation. So we do this by prescribing a host of rules—I call them the "thou-shalt-nots" of the organization. They reside in the company policy manual, which is often several inches thick. These policies try to limit behavior. For example, only certain people can spend company money, and then only up to a certain limit. Employees are not to place various body parts in the factory equipment, so that they might lose those body parts. If they violate this rule, the company will not be held liable.

The problem with rules is that they are only obeyed by people who agree with them. Those who do not will simply find a way to circumvent the rules. When they are caught, they often plead ignorance. So, as Tom Peters has pointed out in *Thriving On Chaos* (1987), there is no way in which policies control the behavior of employees.

The proper way to reduce the variability of behavior in an organization is to use a positive approach—to have a clear vision and mission for people to achieve. And to have a plan that shows how that mission will be achieved.

*The proper way to reduce variability of behavior is to have a clear **vision** and **mission**.*

The question is, does a "one-size-fits-all" style of leadership work? If not, how much variation is acceptable and under what conditions is such variation appropriate?

3

Personality and Leadership

It seems intuitively obvious that a person would lead people in accordance with his or her personality characteristics. Furthermore, since human beings exhibit an almost unlimited variety of personalities, it would seem that there also would be an unlimited variety of leadership styles.

Swiss psychiatrist Carl Jung studied personality and proposed that there are four dimensions or attributes that combine to yield 16 broad personality "types." Based on this theory, Myers and Briggs developed the well-known personality instrument called the Myers-Briggs Type Indicator, or MBTI. About one million individuals take the MBTI each year in the United States, making it one of the most widely used instruments in the total arsenal of psychological measuring devices.

Extroverts are energized by interacting with the "outside" world—the world of objects, people, or animals.

THE JUNG DIMENSIONS

There are four "scales" in the Jung theory:

- Extroversion–Introversion
- Sensing–Intuition
- Thinking–Feeling
- Judging–Perceiving

Extroversion–Introversion

This scale deals with how we are energized. Extroverts are energized by interacting with the "outside" world—the world of concrete objects, people, or animals. Introverts are energized by the "inside" world of concepts, thoughts, or ideas. One way to think about this is to consider what excites people. Extroverts become excited by things outside themselves. Introverts get excited by thoughts and ideas. The terms *extrovert* and *introvert* do not mean that one is outgoing and the other a hermit. There are many introverts who enjoy interacting with people, but they may prefer that the interaction be a sharing of ideas, thoughts, and so on, whereas the extrovert may enjoy just

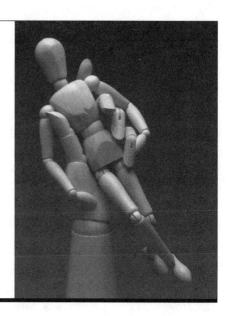

*Introverts are
energized by the
"inside" world
of concepts,
thoughts, or
ideas.*

making conversation about almost any subject. Introverts may well be bored by conversations that are mostly "small talk," because such discussion does not energize them.

Sensing–Intuition

Sensing–Intuition describes how people prefer to take in information—focused on what is real and actual or on patterns and meanings in data. A sensing person just wants the "facts." No doubt the detective Joe Friday was a sensing person because he was famous for saying, "Just the facts, ma'am, just the facts." The person who takes in information through intuition sees patterns and meaning in those facts. We might say that the intuitive person *interprets,* while the sensing person simply *reads* the data.

Thinking–Feeling

This scale is about how people prefer to make decisions. Thinking people make decisions based on logical analysis, and feeling people are guided by their concern for the impact on others. Those with a preference for thinking may make decisions in organizations based

29

almost exclusively on economics, while those who prefer feeling will think more about how the decision will affect other employees. It is important to understand that the thinker is not a cold, uncaring person. He or she may actually say that if economics are not considered, it will be bad for everyone. This is certainly the case when a company must lay off a large number of the workforce to survive. Perhaps the Star Trek saying could be applied to this thinking: "The good of the many outweighs the good of the one."

Judging–Perceiving

This scale describes how people prefer to deal with the outside world—in a planned, orderly way or in a flexible, spontaneous way. The "judgers" are the natural time managers, planners, and organizers. The "perceivers" are more likely to be poor at these activities. They don't particularly like schedules—they prefer to keep their options open, to "roll with the punches." As you can imagine, when these two interact, there may be fireworks. The perceiver may never be on time, which may drive the judger crazy.

I consider these terms to be an unfortunate choice of words. Judging suggests evaluating others—perhaps in a harsh way. And perceiving suggests perhaps being more aware of the world than other people. Nevertheless, we are stuck with them since they have been used for a long time, so I suggest you be careful to understand the true meanings of the words used in this context.

Temperaments

Now by combining these four scales, you arrive at 16 personality types. The difficulty with the personality types is that even 16 of them can be overwhelming to keep straight in one's mind. Fortunately, there is a simplification, known as temperaments.

Temperament is a predisposition to behave in certain ways, and according to Dr. David Keirsey (1998) was first outlined by Hippocrates about 370 B.C. and was further refined by the Roman physician Galen around 190 A.D. Over the years, temperaments have been given a lot of names—sanguine, melancholic, choleric, and phlegmatic being a few.

In a manner similar to Jung, Keirsey determined that two dimensions combine to yield four personality temperaments. One dimension is the way in which a person communicates, the bipolar ends being *abstract* and *concrete*. The other dimension is the manner in which a person uses tools, the poles being *cooperative* and *utilitarian*. Of course, these words anchor the extreme ends of what would clearly be a continuous scale of cooperation or communication abstractness, so that again you would have an almost unlimited variety of combinations. In fact, this is why all attempts to precisely categorize people must ultimately fail, because the variety is truly infinite, and people simply refuse to be pigeon-holed into exact descriptive categories. Nevertheless, it is certainly helpful to simplify, so we will sacrifice precision for the benefit of convenience.

Before discussing the combinations, we should first explain what is meant by the terms. Communication that is concrete is very precise, consisting of words that convey signals to others. Abstract communication, however, conveys symbols that stand for something. Concrete communication would convey something you could see, hear, taste, touch, or smell—that is, it is sensory-oriented. Abstract communication would evoke ideas in the mind, things that do not have concrete existence in the outer world— ideas or concepts such as love, justice, fairness, and so on.

Cooperative versus utilitarian use of tools to accomplish a person's goals needs clarification on several grounds. First, the word *tool* is very broad in this context. Almost everything we do to achieve a goal requires that we use tools of some kind, and Keirsey uses the word to mean everything from a screwdriver to an automobile or house. Some are clearly simple, and others are highly complex.

When we say that a person uses tools cooperatively, we mean that he or she will use a tool in a way that is considered "correct" by most members of society. The person who uses tools in a utilitarian manner will, on the other hand, use the tool he considers best for the job, regardless of whether most people would approve. If all he has is a screwdriver and he needs to jack up a car, that's what he will use. It is not that such an individual does not care about the approval of others—it is a matter of priority, and achieving the goal comes before approval in his scheme of things.

Before we go any further, if you would like to take either the Myers-Briggs or the Keirsey Temperament Sorter, you can do so online. Here are the urls: http://www.keirsey.com/ and http://www.cpp-db.com/.

The Four Temperaments

Since you have two poles on each factor, you get four combinations of them. These are shown in Figure 3.1. Each two-letter code is extracted from the larger four-letter personality type described by Myers-Briggs. Each temperament also has a name, as shown in the figure.

As of April 5, 2002, the Keirsey Web site listed results for 6,267,503 individuals who had taken the Keirsey Temperament Sorter, which is Keirsey's own instrument for measuring psychological types. The percentages that are given for each temperament in the following sections were taken from the Keirsey Web site. Later, I will show a comparison of this data for people who have taken the Myers-Briggs Type Indicator, as the two instruments yield slightly different percentages.

The NF or Idealist Temperament

In the upper left corner of the model shown in Figure 3.1, we have the NF temperament, which Keirsey calls the Idealist. Gandhi was an idealist leader. Idealists represent about 30 percent of the population, according to Keirsey. Abstract in their communication and cooperative in their use of tools, the idealist leader tends to exhort followers to pursue great dreams together. Many of them have a spiritual leaning, as did Gandhi, who also advocated nonviolent protest and resistance to domination by the British.

The NT or Rational Temperament

In the lower left corner, we find the NT temperament, also called the Rationals by Keirsey. These people are abstract in their communication and uncooperative in their use of tools. Remember, *uncooperative* simply means that they don't feel bound by conven-

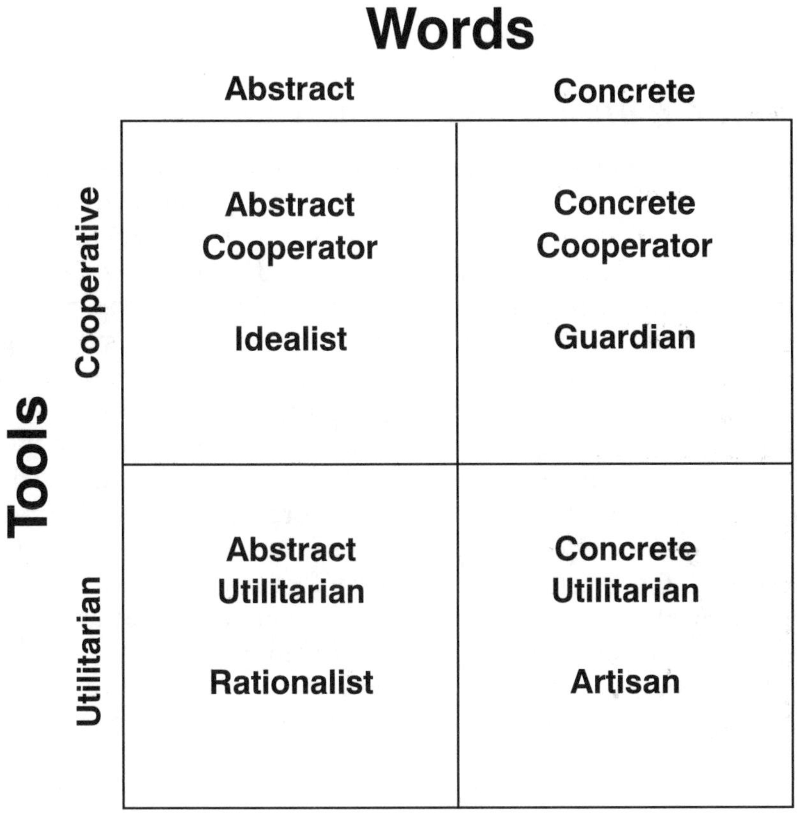

Words

	Abstract	Concrete
Cooperative	Abstract Cooperator Idealist	Concrete Cooperator Guardian
Utilitarian	Abstract Utilitarian Rationalist	Concrete Utilitarian Artisan

(left axis: **Tools**)

Figure 3.1
The personality temperaments.

tion. As a simple example, if all they have is a screwdriver and they need to jack up a car, they may try to use the screwdriver to do so. A cooperative tool user would never dream of doing such a thing!

Keirsey believes that Thomas Jefferson was a rational president. Jefferson had a strong interest in science, as do many rationals. He supported the Lewis and Clark expedition and was intrigued by the fossil specimens that they brought back. He also designed Monticello, which is truly an innovative structure available for tour in Charlottesville, Virginia.

There are a lot of engineers, programmers, and other science and technical individuals who are Rationals. Rationals represent about 14 percent of the population, according to Keirsey.

The Guardian or SJ Temperament

The upper right corner of the matrix contains the SJ temperament, which Keirsey calls the Guardian. This temperament represents about 44 percent of the population, and is the temperament of many business managers, educators, and administrators. These individuals are concrete in their communication and cooperative in their use of tools. They tend to believe strongly in rules and regulations. You should *never* use a tool in an unconventional way. They tend to be good organizers, good planners, and very structured. Interestingly, the Guardians and Rationals make up only 45 percent of the total population, but Keirsey has observed that they comprise nearly 80 percent of most corporations. Furthermore, since they are diagonally across from each other in the matrix, they have the greatest chance for conflict because their mode of communication is opposite (abstract versus concrete) as is their use of tools (cooperative versus uncooperative).

I find this basis of conflict to be valid in organizations. Many NT engineers find themselves in conflict with SJ managers who "just don't understand" them. The engineer is trying to sell some lofty (abstract) technical concept to the manager who doesn't grasp it, complaining that he or she wishes the engineer would speak in (concrete) down-to-earth language that makes business (call that monetary) sense. On top of that, the engineers have no respect for corporate rules and regulations. They want to do untried and unproven things, which drives the SJ manager crazy!

The Artisan or SP

Finally, the lower right corner of the matrix is home for the artisans. The population consists of about 13 percent Artisans. However, there are very few of them in conventional corporations. They can't stand the restrictions of bureaucratic structures. As the name implies, they tend to be artistic in their nature, and being uncooperative in their use of tools, they dislike rules and regulations. So they tend to be independent craftspeople—perhaps carpenters, potters, sculptors, woodworkers, musicians, and so on.

NF (32.9/30.1)				SJ (36.5/43.5)			
TYPE	MBTI	KEIRSEY	TOTAL	TYPE	MBTI	KEIRSEY	TOTAL
INFP	11.4	6.8	22.7/15.4	ISFJ	12.0	9.7	20.6/21.9
ENFP	11.3	8.6		ESFJ	8.6	12.2	
INFJ	5.9	7.3	10.2/14.7	ISTJ	8.8	10.6	15.9/21.6
ENFJ	4.3	7.4		ESTJ	7.1	11.0	
NT (12.7/13.7)				SP (17.2/12.7)			
TYPE	MBTI	KEIRSEY	TOTAL	TYPE	MBTI	KEIRSEY	TOTAL
INTP	4.0	3.1	7.6/5.3	ISFP	5.9	3.0	11.3/7.8
ENTP	3.6	2.2		ESFP	5.4	4.8	
INTJ	2.9	5.2	5.1/8.4	ISTP	3.1	2.2	5.9/4.9
ENTJ	2.2	3.2		ESTP	2.8	2.7	

Table 3.1
Population distribution of types.

Temperament and Type Population Distribution

Two Web sites list the percentage of each type found in the population. One is based on the Keirsey Temperament Sorter and the other on the Myers-Briggs. Since these two instruments can be expected to be just a little different, you would expect the percentages to be different, and they are. Of course, there should be general agreement, or you must question the construct validity of each instrument—that is, do they really measure the same thing?

The other issue is that people who go to Web sites do not necessarily represent the population as a whole. So we must be careful not to credit too much accuracy to the data. However, the Keirsey site has data for 6,267,503 individuals and the MBTI site has data for 20,000, so I believe it is safe to say that these figures are pretty reliable.

Table 3.1 shows the population percentages for each type grouped under its temperament. This table shows that NTs account for about 30 percent of the population, NFs about 13 percent, SJs around 40 percent, and SPs make up the remaining 17 percent.

Keirsey says that, although the SJ and NT groups make only about 50 percent of the population, they account for about 80 percent of corporate populations. One reason may be that Artisans (SPs) tend to leave organizations that are very bureaucratic (which is typical of corporations), and many in the NF category go into teaching, so they too are absent from corporations in great numbers.

Population Distributions at Work

For many years, Otto Kroeger has been specializing in using the Myers-Briggs for helping organizations improve performance. In his book, *Type Talk at Work* (Kroeger and Thuesen, 1992), he and his co-author provide statistics for the distribution of the types in the workplace. While they present the breakdown for all 16 types, I think it is instructive to look at these for the temperaments. Five categories are listed. Notice the striking differences you see in the various jobs, especially in the climb from management to executive level. (See Table 3.2. Note that because of rounding, the percentages do not always total exactly 100.0%.)

This table is extremely compelling in showing that temperament affects career paths. You will note that the Idealists and Artisans are almost absent from the executive ranks, which are dominated by the Guardians and Rationals. In the remainder of this chapter and in the next chapter, we will see that this has a profound meaning for how organizations are managed.

What is really striking, and is not shown here, is that for executives, if you look at all 16 types, you find that among the SJ category, the SFJ types represent only 1.4 percent and the STJ comprise the remaining 60.1 percent. That is, the feeling component of one's type is a detriment to climbing to the top of the corporate ladder. (You can also see this in the absence of NF temperaments at the top.) In addition, if you examine the JP dimension among the NT group, you find that the NTP subgroup represents only 6.6 percent of the total, with the NTJ subgroup accounting for the remaining 25.2 percent. This suggests that companies give more "credit" to those managers whose feelings don't greatly affect their decisions, but who use thinking as the basis for them.

Job	Number	NF	NT	SJ	SP
Entry level	1320	13.0%	9.0%	51.0%	27.0%
Mid management	4789	6.0%	29.0%	55.0%	10.0%
Upper management	5300	3.6%	43.0%	47.0%	7.0%
Executives	2245	2.1%	32.0%	62.0%	4.6%
Training personnel	2951	40.0%	31.0%	24.0%	5.0%

Table 3.2
Population distribution of the temperaments in the workplace (adapted from Kroeger and Thuesen, 1992).

Temperament and Managerial Intelligence

Keirsey has a unique view of intelligence, one that departs from conventional thinking on the subject. He says, ". . . I base my type definitions on what people do well, their skilled actions—what I call their 'intelligent roles'—which are observable, and which can be defined . . . objectively" (1998). He then says, "Common sense tells us that intelligence is being smart in what we do. In other words, it is not how well we think, but how well we act in a given role. If our behavior is adaptive to circumstances, so that we act effectively in such circumstances, then we can be said to be intelligent in those circumstances." Given this perspective on intelligence, Keirsey writes, "What is the relationship between temperament and intelligence? The kind of intelligent role enacted by a leader or follower is determined by temperament, and the degree of skill in that role is determined by practice." He goes on to define these four kinds of role intelligences as diplomacy, strategy, tactics, and logistics. For project managers, this is very significant. Each will tend to excel at one of the four roles as a function of his or her temperament.

The NF (Idealist) project manager will usually be best at diplomacy. The NT Rational will excel at strategy. The SP Artisan will be good at tactics. And the SJ Guardian will be strong in logistics. However, it is not an all-or-nothing proposition because you seldom find pure types, much less pure temperaments, and because each of us has some preferences for each dimension of the four scales, we would expect that each individual would be

Common sense tells us that intelligence is being smart in what we do. It is not how well we think, but how well we act in a given role.

able to exercise all four kinds of role intelligence. It is just a matter of degree.

If we take the temperament matrix and rearrange it as shown in Table 3.3, we see that going around the matrix in the direction indicated will give us the order of strength for each of the temperaments.

Another way to depict the relative strengths of each intelligence is shown in Figure 3.2. Note that this figure shows that the NF–SP and NT–SJ temperaments are mirror images of each other so far as the level of each intelligence is concerned.

Now specifically what does this mean for project managers? The NT project manager (who may often be an engineer, architect, or other technical person) will be best at strategy, about equal in

NF: Diplomacy (clockwise)	NT: Strategy (counterclockwise)
SP: Tactics (counterclockwise)	SJ: Logistics (clockwise)

Table 3.3
Temperaments and role intelligence.

38

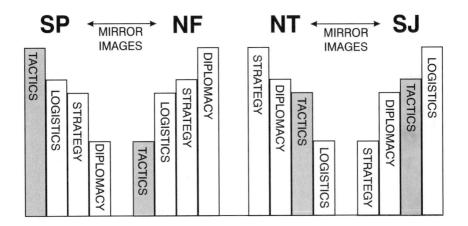

Figure 3.2
Temperament and intelligence.

diplomacy and tactics, and not so good at logistics. The SJ project manager (typical of general managers in corporations) will be very good at logistics, about equal in tactics and diplomacy, and not so good at strategy.

Remember that the temperaments and types are preferences, not abilities, but that there is a correlation. When one has a preference for something, he or she tends to engage in that activity a lot, and therefore develops skill in it. It is likely, then, that the foregoing paragraph will be true, although there will always be exceptions to it. For one thing, we know that most people do not score as all intuitive or all sensing, but somewhere along a continuum, so that they will be a little intuitive even though their strong preference is sensing. So the NF may have enough SP in himself that he is excellent at strategy and better at logistics than would be expected (logistics supposedly being his least skilled role).

APPLYING THIS TO PROJECT MANAGEMENT

Now let's see how this can be applied to project management. Over the years, I developed a model for managing projects which I call the Lewis Method®. This model is portrayed as a flow chart, showing the sequence in which various steps are taken to manage a project. The model is shown in Figure 3.3. As you can see, there are five phases in my model of a project: Definition, Planning Strategy, Implementation Planning, Execution and Control, and Closeout.

Let's begin at the definition phase, which is where many projects get off to a bad start. Since a project begins as a concept—just a fuzzy notion in someone's mind—the first thing that must be done is to clarify exactly what the project will accomplish. What results is it expected to achieve, what must be delivered to get those results, and what expectations do various stakeholders have for the outcomes of the project?

Part of this process requires analytical skills, which would usually be possessed by very left-brained individuals, those with a strong preference for thinking (so this would include the ISTJ, ESTJ, ISTP, and ESTP types, as well as the INTP, ENTP, INTJ, and ENTJ types). In other words, the NF temperaments would generally be excluded along with two of the types that fall in the SP category (ISFP and ESFP). Altogether, they amount to about 40 percent of the population, but they also come from the two groups least represented in most corporations, so we would expect that most individuals would be able to contribute to this step.

Once the definition is developed, project strategy must be formulated. The NT is the clear choice to contribute in this case, and we are in luck because they represent a fairly substantial percentage of most corporate populations. Note that it is not necessarily the project manager who must develop strategy, but if he or she is not an NT temperament, then an NT team member must be enlisted to take charge of this part of the project-planning stage.

Next comes implementation planning, which will consist of planning tactics and logistics. For this, the SJ and SP temperaments will tend to excel. Unfortunately, since we are likely to find an absence of SP (Artisans) in most organizations, we may have to rely on the SJs to deal with both tactics and logistics. They will usually be stronger in logistics than tactics, but the NTs may be able to contribute to tactics, so all is not lost.

During execution and control, we will need strong support from the SJs because many of the issues will be about logistics, at

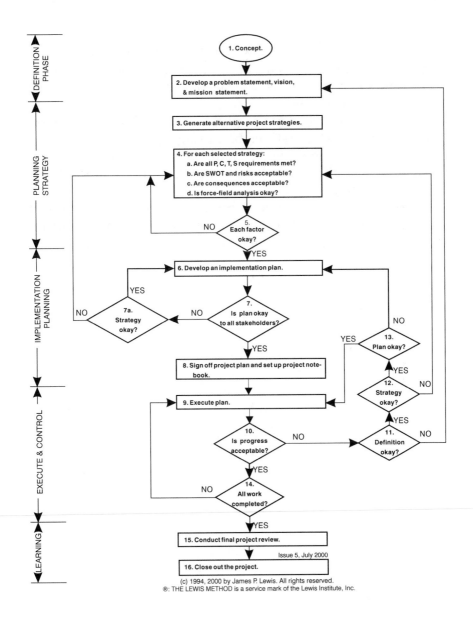

Figure 3.3
The Lewis Method of project management.

41

which they tend to excel. However, the situation now becomes very dynamic, and you may find that under stress you need a leader with diplomatic skills, which would mean the NFs with the NTs being a close second.

Finally, during the closeout phase, you need a mix of skills. You need diplomacy to ask "embarrassing" questions—What was done well? What should we try to do better next time? You also need some analytical skills, which the NT and SJ temperaments will probably be pretty good at.

These are some of the issues. But only some of them. We will see in the next chapter that it is the interactions among temperaments that is perhaps most important.

4

Temperament and Motivation

*N*ot only are we motivated to behave in ways that satisfy our needs but to pursue our interests as well. Each temperament has different interests and motivations. Table 4.1 is a brief summary of these, taken from Keirsey (1998, p. 128).

Before we go further, it may be helpful to remind ourselves that there are very few individuals who are *pure* temperaments. For example, my Keirsey Temperament Sorter scores for T and F are 5 points for T and 15 for F. For that reason, I have some characteristics of both the NF and NT, with NF being stronger. However, you will note that I first became an engineer (characteristic of the NT), although I always had an interest in people. Eventually my interest in people "won out" over my technical interests (and I got a Ph.D. in psychology) although I still love to read about science and technology.

Interests	Idealists	Artisans	Guardians	Rationals
Educational	Humanities	Arts & Crafts	Commerce	Sciences
Preoccupation	Morale	Techniques	Morality	Technology
Vocational	Personnel	Equipment	Materiel	Systems

Table 4.1

INTERESTS OF THE TEMPERAMENTS

Interests of Idealists (NFs)

Idealists are drawn to the humanities, especially to professions that involve communicating ideas using words. They enjoy communicating with people. If they work at it, they usually become very proficient at writing, and many of them become teachers of literature.

The humanities do not just consist of literature, however, so many Idealists find themselves drawn to the social sciences, particularly the fields of mental healing, and personal or religious counseling (Keirsey, 1998, p. 130). In fact, the motivation of many NF individuals is to be helpers. They also tend to be strongly into *self-actualization,* a term Abraham Maslow used to mean that they are motivated to fully express themselves. To use the slogan heard in many U. S. Army recruitment commercials, self-actualization is to "Be all that you can be."

Idealists are also concerned about morale—with the feelings of worth that others have—that is, with their self-image, their self-respect, self-esteem, and self-confidence. They are concerned that people in teams have high morale and when decisions are made, the NF is likely to weigh very heavily how the decision will affect the feelings of others. It is here that a conflict may exist between the NF and NT, with the NT being more concerned about economic or technical issues, the NF about feelings. In the extreme, the NF may be viewed as a "bleeding heart," and the NT as cold and uncaring. Neither extreme is likely to be true, of course.

When an NF individual finds a job in personnel, you can be sure that the needs of people will be placed high on the priority list. They will be strong advocates for human resource development, for treating people fairly, for eliminating sexual harassment

Idealists (NFs)

Idealists are drawn to the humanities. They communicate ideas using words. They are concerned with the feelings of others.

on the job, and for generally helping people find a rewarding home in the workplace. However, many human resource administrators are Guardians (just as many managers are), and while these people are not uncaring, they do not express the same concern for people as do the Idealists. In fact, many employees who go to personnel seeking counseling or some other form of personal help find that they do not receive the caring response that they expected because the guardian administrator simply does not fit the counselor mold as well as the NF does.

Interests of Artisans (SPs)

Since the Artisans are diagonally across from the Idealists on the Keirsey matrix, we could expect them to have very different interests as well, and they do. In school they tend to head for the arts and crafts and stay away from the humanities and sciences. They are, in fact, often bored by the guardian-oriented tone of school curricula and try to relieve their boredom in ways that teachers often find disruptive. It is these children who are often diagnosed as being hyperactive and placed on drugs to control their behavior. Since they represent about 17 percent of the population, this is a significant number of children.

Artisans (SPs)

Artisans are driven to master techniques. They head for the arts and enjoy speech-making and making deals.

In any event, arts and crafts isn't just about painting or sculpting. It also includes athletics; cooking; literary, martial, mechanical, theatrical, and industrial arts; and as Donald Trump has called it, the "art of the deal" in business. Artisans tend to excel in any of these.

Artisans are really driven to master techniques. Note that we are not saying technology, which they may actually avoid. Techniques include playing musical instruments, painting, sculpting, catching, kicking, throwing, and using various instruments. Surfers are a great example. Whether it be speech making, making deals, or woodworking, the SP is drawn to techniques like a fly to honey.

They do love working with all kinds of equipment. They must drive race cars, pilot planes, steer boats, wield scalpels, and so on. Keirsey speculates that in prehistoric times the "Artisans must have been the chief hunters and the finest warriors. The sling, the club, the spear, the bow and arrow; these equipped the SP tribesmen for their deadly art" (Keirsey, 1998, p. 45).

Interests of Rationals (NTs)

Unlike the Idealists and Artisans, who tend to avoid the sciences, the Rationals are drawn to them. However, they avoid the humanities, where the other two temperaments are very attuned to

*Rationals
(NTs)*

---

*Rationals are
drawn to the
sciences and it
can engage
them in lifelong
study.*

Shooting for the moon
—making action plans

them. Keirsey says that Rationals should work with systems, rather than with materiel, tools, or personnel (Keirsey, 1998).

He goes on to say,

*materiel: military supplies and equipment
material: something used to make items*

> Long ago Rationals were the tribal sorcerers, attempting to bend nature to their will; later, in medieval times, they were the alchemists seeking the philosopher's stone. Today, the largely clerical curriculum in most elementary and secondary schools is boring to NTs, simply because it is wrong for them. What arouses their inherent curiosity is the work of science—logical investigation, critical experimentation, mathematical description—and it can engage and absorb them in lifelong study (Keirsey, 1998, pp. 176–177).

The Rationals are preoccupied with technology, which can be thought of as the "logic of building," whereas the Artisans are concerned with the "skill of building." The Rationals may design the building, but the Artisans will construct it. In fact, Rationals may be either engineers or architects.

They are intrigued by machines and organisms. Organisms are studied by anthropologists, biologists, ethnologists, psychologists,

47

and sociologists, while machines are studied by engineers of all kinds. The complexity of these organic and machine systems fascinates Rationals.

Interests of Guardians (SJs)

Although the Guardians and Rationals comprise only 50-odd percent of the population, Keirsey believes that they make up about 80 percent of corporate populations. This is interesting because they are diagonally opposite each other in the temperament matrix. The Guardians are cooperative in their use of tools and concrete in their communication, while the Rationals are utilitarian in using tools and abstract in their communication. And naturally, their interests are also diametrically opposite.

The Guardians are very concerned about morality—not morale—the right and wrong way to behave. They are drawn to commerce and may have an aversion to technology. The Rationals are just the opposite, so you can expect friction—indeed significant conflict between these two temperaments—and that is exactly my experience with them. They have difficulty communicating—the Guardian preferring concrete, fact-based statements, while the Rationals are talking in abstract terms about concepts, the big picture, system interactions, and so on. The Guardian wants to see rules observed—especially rules concerning the use of tools (remember, this means anything from a real tool to an automobile), and the Rationals think rules are for mere mortals perhaps, but not for themselves.

Then there is the clash over commerce versus technology. I have worked with NT engineers who have no sense of project budget concerns or deadlines. They are in pursuit of the dream of creating a perfect machine, and damn the schedule! They complain bitterly that insisting on meeting deadlines means that they cannot do a *good* job. They really mean that they can't make it perfect although of course, by definition, perfection is unachievable. They have a very hard time "satisficing"—making it "good enough" for the present, then coming back later to improve it. If you left the release of new products to the perfec-

Guardians (SJs)

Keirsey says that guardians make up about 80% of corporate populations. The guardians excel in logistics and are natural organizers.

tionist engineers, products would never get released because these engineers could always find a way to make them better.

What the Guardians really excel at is logistics—the handling of materiel, military equipment, and supplies. Here again there is a source of conflict with the Rational, who is a natural strategic thinker, seeing the big picture, the grand game plan, while the Guardian is thinking about the "nitty-gritty" details of "feeding" the troops who must execute this great plan. Interestingly, the Germans learned the hard way during World War II just how important logistics is when they got their troops into Africa and couldn't fight because they had no ammunition and other supplies.

Guardians are the natural organizers. They love occupations that deal with managing materiel, organizing things, scheduling, keeping things running smoothly, and keeping records. They are stabilizers, trying to keep the ship on an even keel, while the NT Rationals want to change the direction of the ship. In fact, visionary leaders often find that the Guardian middle managers may block the very change in procedures that they (the Visionaries) are trying to implement. This is not deliberate sabotage, however. The Guardian was hired to do exactly that—to stabilize things.

MOTIVATION PATTERNS

I have already said that we are motivated to satisfy our needs, and that these fall into five broad categories. It is also true that each person has his or her own way of doing this—by engaging in a certain pattern of activity. Some examples of such patterns include innovation, being an expert, troubleshooting, learning, self-development, helping, organizing, defending, and teaching. It seems natural that each temperament might be drawn to a particular pattern of activity, based on the typical interests that they have.

For example, I would expect that many Guardians would be defenders and organizers. Defenders are those who are very concerned with ensuring that rules, regulations, and procedures are followed. The stereotype is the bureaucrat, and indeed, there is no doubt that many bureaucrats are Guardians.

The NF Idealists are definitely motivated to be helpers. They frequently find careers in the helping professions, which I believe includes being professional diplomats, which is their natural intelligence. They are also drawn to self-development, but of a special type—often involving spiritual pursuits, making themselves better human beings. The NT may also be a writer or teacher. If a writer, they may be innovative in the use of words. As teachers (which may be thought of as a helping profession) they may also be innovative, like Jaime Escalante, which can arouse the indignation of the more traditional SJ teachers (which is what happened to Escalante).

The Artisans love mastering techniques, which can be thought of as self-development, but which could also be thought of as making themselves master craftspersons. They may also enjoy troubleshooting.

The NT Rationals clearly are drawn to innovating. These intuitive thinkers love system design, creating beautiful buildings, and other such pursuits. They may also be experts, reveling in filling their heads full of information, and having people ask questions that they can answer. They tend to be lifelong learners, as stated earlier, studying science and technology.

It is actually fairly easy to determine the pattern of activity that motivates an individual. The reason is that these patterns are repetitive. That is, we tend to engage in the same pattern of activity every time we are motivated, so the key is to examine situations in which people are motivated and determine what they are doing.

Begin With a Job

To do this, I go through the following procedure. I ask the person to tell me about a time when he (to avoid the awkward construction he or she throughout this, I am going to use he exclusively) was involved in a job that really "turned him on." "It was a job that you really enjoyed, looked forward to doing, perhaps thought about a lot on your way to work," I say. "Do you remember something like that?"

Usually every person can tell me about at least one work experience that was motivating, but if he can't I switch to another category, or I may ask him to describe the ideal job. What would it be like? What would he be doing in it—that is, what part would he play?

As the person tells me about the job experience, I make mental notes. You have to listen very carefully, so you remember almost every detail.

Then Ask About a Hobby or Sport

Then I ask him to tell me about some outside activity he engages in. It must be an activity, not some vegetative thing, like lying on the beach in the sun. That is not a motivator (as an activity) but a mode of relaxation . I'm looking for a hobby or sport. Perhaps golf or tennis or woodworking.

Here you must be specific about what the person does in this activity. For example, I have known individuals who would just as soon play golf alone. I can almost guarantee that such individuals are Artisans, who care only about perfecting their skill (technique) at the game. The social aspect does not interest them whatsoever.

On the other hand, there are those who wouldn't dream of playing golf alone. Golf, for these individuals, is a social thing, and the score isn't as important as the social component. No doubt these are Extroverts (who draw energy from the outside world) and for whom the pattern of activity may simply be social interaction.

Then there are those who are so highly competitive that they, too, could not play golf alone, because their objective is the destruction of the competitor. For them, it is not "how you play the game" that counts. Winning is everything. Their pattern of activity is proving that they are better than others.

Next, Ask About a Fantasy or Dream

Now I ask the person to tell me about something he has always wanted to do but has never gotten to do. I refer to it as a fantasy or dream—something from his "wish list." Many people tell me they would like to travel. Here again, you must get specific information. "Would you prefer to see four cities in three days or stay in one place for a week? Would you want to spend time living with a local family or just sight-seeing. Do you prefer sight-seeing with an organized tour or strictly on your own?"

I sometimes ask, "What's the big deal? What do you think you would get out of it?" The answers to such questions tell you a lot about what motivates the person.

Now Look for the Pattern

Once you have these three activities, you will find that there is a thread that runs through them. Every single one will contain the same pattern of activity. It is not the *content* of the activity that matters but what the person *does* with the content that counts.

When you are learning to do this, it helps to do it in a group of three. The third person can help you process the data you have obtained from the interviewee. Then you can rotate, so that each of you gets to interview, be interviewed, and be a helper.

You will find that most people do not have entirely pure patterns. For example, I am a helper/innovator. I love to create something new—and if it is something that will help people as well, then I get a double payback. I also use teaching as my helping profession. I could be a clinical psychologist, and would enjoy it, but I

Project management has been linked to herding cats.

But cats don't herd very well; they are very independent, much like members of project teams.

can reach far more people through writing and teaching, so that is my approach to helping.

However, I started out as an engineer, and designing communications equipment was my true love. That was the NT component of my personality coming through because I am part T and part F, with F being stronger. So I share some motivation with both temperaments. You probably will find that most people are like this, unless their T–F, J–P, and S–N scores are off the scale in one direction—that is, the person is all T or all F, all J or all P, and so on. You seldom find this, however.

WHAT THIS MEANS FOR PROJECT LEADERS

Project management has been likened to herding cats. Anyone who knows cats can immediately appreciate the irony. Cats don't herd very well. They are very independent creatures. I happen to like cats a lot, and I have firsthand experience that validates this assertion. And it is true that members of project teams seem like a bunch of cats, each going in his or her own direction, refusing to follow your lead. Why is this?

Well, it could be that you are lucky enough to have a team consisting of all of the temperaments. It is, of course, a mixed blessing. On the one hand, diversity brings strength to any problem-solving team. On the other, that diversity makes it exceedingly hard to reach agreement on anything.

Most importantly, however, it may be that you are not engaging the person in the motivation pattern that fits his or her temperament. If, for example, you try to make an NT do detailed logistics work, you are going to destroy his or her motivation. Remember, the SJ is the logistics person, and the NT is a strategy person.

The Leader's Job

I have said that leadership is the art of getting others to want to do something you want them to do. Keirsey has a nice way of defining the job. He says, "The leader's objective, whatever his or her temperament, is to execute a plan of operations in the pursuit of a specified goal" (Keirsey, 1998, p. 287). He goes on to say that achieving a goal requires a certain kind and degree of intelligence, so that leaders must take into account their own intelligence, as well as that of their followers. Since various facets of a complex project will require different kinds of intelligence, the job for a project manager is to mach talent to task.

This makes sense so far as task performance is concerned, but there is the motivation aspect as well. As I have said, you are only a leader if you have followers, and you will only have willing followers if you are taking them somewhere that they want to go and if you are helping them meet their needs in the process.

Now one of the strong needs that all human beings have is to be approved of by others—especially their leaders. So one of the acts that is more important to a leader than almost anything is to show followers that they are appreciated.

Are a paycheck and the satisfaction of doing a good job not enough? No. This is not to say that they are unimportant. They

We want to be appreciated in proportion to our contribution, from the person in charge, in addition to a paycheck and job satisfaction.

just aren't enough. We all want appreciation, and we want it from the person in charge. Furthermore, we want to be appreciated in proportion to our contribution. It also turns out that the big contributors also have the greatest appetite for appreciation. As Keirsey puts it, "Achievement generates appreciation hunger" (Keirsey, 1998, p. 288).

I have often had this discussion with managers who feel that the need to express appreciation to employees is just "touchy-feely" stuff. "They're getting paid to do the work," protest some managers. "Why should I have to tell them I appreciate it?"

These managers are clueless about people. And there are a lot of them, apparently. Many employees have confided to me that their bosses don't seem to appreciate what they do—that they are taken for granted. And you can bet that if you follow those high achievers whose bosses fail to show appreciation for their contributions, sooner or later they will leave the job in search of a place where their work is appreciated.

Now remember that each temperament has high intelligence in one of the four categories: strategy, diplomacy, logistics, or tactics. That means their best performance tends to be in terms of one of these. It also means that leaders must express appreciation for high performance in that person's intelligence. So, for example, the NT is highest in strategy. He or she will tend to make the greatest contribution in matters dealing with the big picture, with systems, and in creating new products, buildings, or organisms. So they also want to be appreciated for those contributions.

Here's the catch: Leaders have difficulty appreciating the intelligence of temperaments other than their own. The Guardian leader, whose strong suit is logistics, has difficulty appreciating the strategy contribution of the Rational. This is probably one reason why engineers hate being led by non-engineers. The non-engineer is likely to be a Guardian, given that about 55 percent of mid-level managers are of this temperament. And this being the case, the guardian manager does not appreciate the contributions of the rational engineer.

Does this mean that engineers really should be led only by other engineers? No, I don't believe so. What it does mean is that every leader must learn to understand the characteristics of each intelligence and what individuals possessing that intelligence value in terms of appreciation, and they must express that appreciation *sincerely*. I think this is most important. You can't fake appreciation. People sense your lack of sincerity and resent it. So you have a problem. I don't know if you can learn to truly appreciate others if you don't already do so. But perhaps this suggestion will help.

If you recognize that no leader can be a success without the performance of his or her followers, then you recognize that you are totally interdependent as a project team. The team members need your leadership, and you need for them to perform their jobs well. Since your professional success is totally dependent on them, it seems to me that this alone should make you appreciate what they are doing for you. But if you find that you don't really feel any appreciation for your followers, then I have a harsh suggestion: Pursue another career path! You won't be very effective as a leader. Maybe as an administrator, but not as a leader.

Having said that, we now turn to another dimension of people that we must understand to be effective leaders—how people think.

5

You Think Funny!

A *nother dimension* of personal characteristics that every leader
must consider is how people think. Those who think differently,
behave differently, dress differently—in short, people who are different than ourselves—we tend to see as hard to deal with. That is
one reason we are attracted to people similar to ourselves. It is
easy to communicate with them. People who are different are
more difficult.

This accounts in part for the "generation gap" problems that
older people have with younger ones. The kids say, "My parents
and teachers just don't understand me." And it is often true, they
don't, although generally parents understand their kids far better
than the children believe because having been children themselves, parents can empathize with the problems their own kids
are going through.

Relationships

We must find common ground if we are to relate with each other.

The thing is, almost any difference causes others to think they cannot deal with you. And those differences come from age, race, sex, job position, education level and discipline, and so on. In some of my seminars in which I have taught conflict resolution, I have had men tell women that they understand them, and I have seen those women give a nonverbal response that says, "You don't have a clue." To use an extreme example, can you imagine a man telling a mother that he understands how she felt delivering her child? No way!

In addition to the gender difference, I have also seen this in situations in which the parties were of different races—especially African-American and Caucasian. When a white person tells a black person, "I understand where you're coming from," the black individual immediately thinks, "Like hell you do!" And rightfully so. It is unlikely that a white person has had the same life experience as an African American. Similarly, unless you have been poor, you can't relate to that experience. Which is why therapists who have never suffered a particular problem cannot truly empathize with their patients, and this in itself makes it more difficult for the therapist to help (which is another story, so we won't go there).

For instance, in spite of the fact that I never grew up in a ghetto, and cannot fully understand the experience of those who did, I have had many problems in my life, and when another person starts telling me about some pain he or she has experienced, if I have suffered from that same pain, I can empathize. We have the basis for a relationship when that happens. I understand what she is going through, and I can at least offer her my shoulder. I may even be able to offer some suggestions for dealing with her pain, if I found one for myself.

So the message is that we must find common ground if we are to relate with each other, and we must understand that we are always more alike than we are different. We must focus on the similarities and discount the differences.

But thinking. That is an entirely different matter. What do you do when someone thinks entirely differently than you do?

THINKING STYLES—THE NED HERRMANN MODEL

At one time, Ned Herrmann was a training manager for General Electric. He had been hearing a lot about the finding that each half of the brain controls different parts of the body and that each side contributes in some way to the way people think. Specifically, the left hemisphere controls (or is the source of) logical thinking, and the right hemisphere is the source of emotion, visualization, and so on.

As he investigated further, Ned decided that this concept was not the entire story. He read more on brain physiology and concluded that a dimension was missing—that of the limbic system and cerebral cortex. With that addition, you have two modes of left-brain thinking and two modes of right-brain thinking. Ned's model is shown in Figure 5.1.

Beginning in quadrant A and going counterclockwise, we have the following general styles. The A quadrant is one in which a person is very logical, analytical, and financially minded. The B quadrant involves an interest in planning and organizing things.

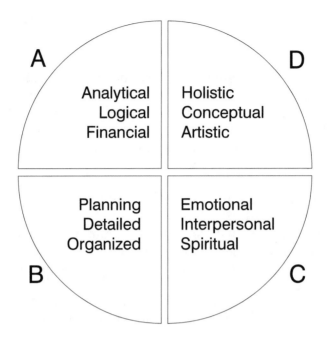

Figure 5.1
The Herrmann thinking model.

This thinking also involves a lot of attention to detail. The financial analysts use A-quadrant thinking, while accountants think in quadrant B. Next, quadrant C involves feeling and emotion, as well as interpersonal thinking and spiritual-mindedness. And finally, quadrant D is holistic, big-picture, conceptual, and artistic in its orientation.

What is important to note is that people have varying degrees of preference for thinking in each of the quadrants, and Ned developed an instrument to measure the strength of a person's preference for thinking in each quadrant. He called this the Herrmann Brain Dominance Instrument (HBDI). As Ned said often, every one of us has a whole brain, but for some reason we don't prefer to use all of it. We *can*, however, so the instrument that Ned developed to measure *preferences* does not measure *ability*. There is a relationship, of course. The stronger one's preference for thinking a certain way, the more one is likely to do so, and that develops skill. So we would expect that, over time, a person will become very proficient at thinking in the preferred quadrants.

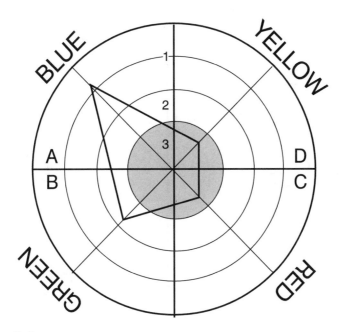

Figure 5.2
HBDI profile of thinking styles.

But how do you indicate strength of preference? Ned began by drawing two axes at 45 degrees to the horizontal. He also placed a scale on each axis. A person's score on the HBDI is then plotted on the scale. Rather than express absolute raw scores, however, Ned decided that it was accurate enough to say that a person scored in the high, medium, or low range on the scale. He did this by drawing concentric circles to place boundaries on each zone. This is shown in Figure 5.2.

You will note that the A quadrant is color-coded blue in Ned's model, the B quadrant is green, C is red, and D is yellow. I have shown a profile on the grid. The person's score in the quadrants is always expressed beginning in quadrant A and rotating counterclockwise, so this profile shows a 1-2-3-3 score. In practice, the hyphens are dropped, so the score would be expressed as 1233.

Figure 5.3 illustrates another profile, this time having a very strong score in quadrant A and weak scores in the other three quadrants. We call this a single-dominant profile, and you will

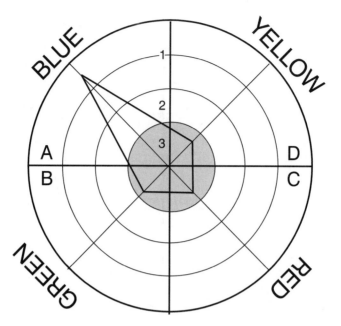

Figure 5.3
Single-dominant profile.

notice that it looks like a kite that you fly on a string, so the generic term for the profile is "kite."

This profile would be labeled 1333. A person having this profile would most likely be strongly analytical in nature—always looking for patterns and meanings in data. She would also probably be seen as somewhat cold since her preference for thinking in the C quadrant is very low. And she would be neither very detailed nor very conceptual. Again, it is not that she *cannot* think in these modes, it is just that she has very little inclination to do so. This means that if you tried to place her in a job requiring such thinking, she would most likely be very unhappy and would probably try to get out of that job as soon as possible. Give her a job requiring analysis, however, and she will be very happy.

Now suppose the person who has a single-dominant A-quadrant profile has to interact with another individual who has an equally strong single-dominant C-quadrant profile—a 3313 profile. What do you suppose will happen? One is strongly analytical and the other is strongly interpersonal.

Well, the A-quadrant person will probably spend a lot of time analyzing the other individual, trying to figure out why she is like she is, and the C-quadrant person will find the A-quadrant individual far too mathematical for her own tastes. There will be very little in common between them, and they would be as likely to form a close friendship as a snowball would have of surviving in a hot oven.

On the other hand, if you put two single-dominant A-quadrant individuals together (or two single-dominant C-quadrant individuals) they would feel *muy simpatico*. For that matter, if you pair a single-dominant person with another person who has strong preference for thinking in that quadrant and all the others, they would still click with each other.

Suppose you saw a profile like the one in Figure 5.4 What prediction would you make about the individual who scored like this? That he is confused? Wishy-washy? Can't make a decision? This profile is called quadruple-dominant. The person has an almost equal preference for thinking in all four quadrants. This means that he would probably develop skill in all four as well.

Such a person would be equally at home talking with other people no matter what quadrant they prefer. Ned Herrmann believed that this is the ideal profile for a CEO, but his research indicates that only a very small percentage of the population has a "square" profile, so you probably won't find too many CEOs with such scores either. The premise is that CEOs must deal with people who have all four thinking preferences, so if he or she feels at home in all four quadrants, then dealing with people of all kinds should be equally easy.

I believe that the ideal profile for a project manager would be a square one for the same reason that it would be good for a CEO, and perhaps even more so. A project manager has little authority and a lot of responsibility in most situations, and in order to get anything done, he or she must use persuasion, influence, and negotiating (begging, even). Most importantly, he or she must deal with people who naturally will fall into all four quadrants, so being able and willing to think in all four of them would be a real asset.

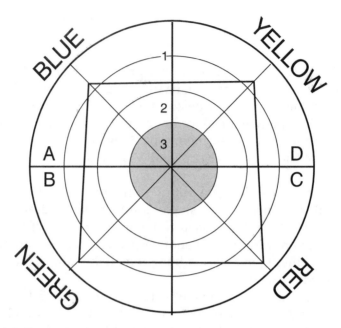

Figure 5.4
Quadruple-dominant profile.

PROJECT TEAMS AND THINKING STYLES

Since complex jobs require all modes of thinking, it seems clear that a team must consist of individuals who can think in all four quadrants. In other words, we want a team that has a "whole brain." Usually with large teams, you will have representation in all four quadrants, but the composite of all the profiles won't necessarily be square, unless it is a *very* large team. As an example, I have seen a composite for a team of technical people that had the shape shown in Figure 5.5. This is a 1131 profile, meaning that, as a team, they have very little inclination to deal with interpersonal things—and this means dealing with "people" issues.

This may be okay on the surface, but if you consider that every team will encounter some interpersonal issues they must deal with, you can bet that this group will have problems, as they have an aversion to thinking interpersonally. So long as they are dealing with technical issues, they will be fine.

Of course, remember that they can think in quadrant C if they choose to do so. This means that if you make them aware of their

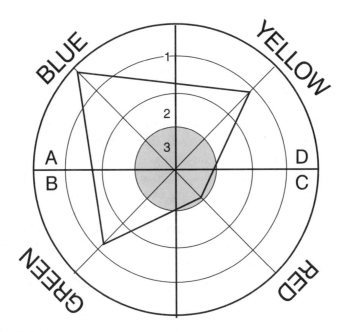

Figure 5.5
A 1131 profile.

tendency to avoid quadrant C, and if you can convince them of the importance of paying attention to that quadrant, then they actually can do it. They may not have the finesse of the single-dominant C-quadrant person we introduced earlier, but they are capable of adequate proficiency.

Problems for the Team

You will remember that I said earlier that differences lead to problems between people. If you are different from me in some way, then I feel that you don't understand me and I don't understand you. This is also true when you "think funny." As I suggested, when I am all quadrant A and you are all quadrant C, we are going to have a tough time communicating.

There is an equally strong conflict between two single-dominant individuals when one is in quadrant B and the other in quadrant D. The D person is a very conceptual, big-picture thinker, while the B person is very detailed, organized, and down-to-earth. The B person will think the D individual is a nut case, always having his head in the clouds, never paying attention to detail; and the D person will think the B individual is so nit-picky that he or she is totally obnoxious. One says the other can't see the forest for the trees, and the other says his opposite can't see the trees for the forest. Either way, they are likely to have a lot of friction between them.

Fortunately most people have multi-dominant profiles, or at least some preference for thinking in all four quadrants, so it is not as bleak a picture as I have painted for the extreme of two single-dominant individuals interacting. I have done this to make you aware of the source of some of the conflicts we have with other people They think differently than we do. That does not make them bad, mad, or crazy, although we are inclined to think they are. It simply means they see the world through a different lens than we do. And thank God that this is true. It would be the most boring world if everyone were the same. (Strictly speaking this is a false statement. If everyone were the same, they would never be unhappy about it because none of them would realize that differences could exist.)

Thinking and Temperaments

An obvious question is whether there is any relationship between the Herrmann model and temperaments, and there is. Studies have found that there is a definite correlation between the four quadrants and two of the Jung scales: the T–F scale and the S–N scale. This is shown in Figure 5.6.

From this, we could expect that the NT Rational would have strong scores in the A and C quadrants, and the NF Idealist would score high in C and D. But what about the SJ and SP temperaments? We don't see the J–P scale represented here. We have a two-dimensional figure here, and it may be that the J–P scale is orthogonal (at a right angle) to this figure. There is a theory that judging is a left-brain function and perceiving is a right-brain function, but this is unproven.

Furthermore, it is hard to know precisely how these scales relate. I have a very good friend whose profile is almost exactly congruent with mine. When you print them on a transparency and

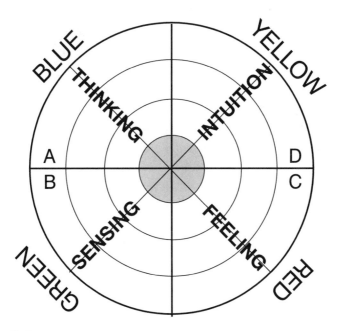

Figure 5.6
HBDI and Jung scales.

lay one on top of the other, you can only see a few points difference on each scale axis. We are both 3211 profiles, as shown in Figure 5.7.

However, in spite of this incredible congruence, he is an NT and I am an NF. As I said earlier, I have enough NT in me to have been an engineer, and it is possible that my thinking preference was stronger back then, but in any event the feeling side of the scale is stronger now. So one of us is an Idealist and the other is a Rational, even though if you judged by the HBDI profiles, you would expect us to be the same.

Part of the explanation lies in how a scale is constructed. The HBDI asks about work preferences and also uses forced-choice word pairs to find which quadrant(s) a person prefers to think in. My friend could have chosen different work items and different words in the pairs and scored the same as I did but have different nuances in his thinking. And that is precisely the truth. We have had many hours of conversation, and while we are more likely to agree than to disagree—especially about significant issues—we certainly are not clones of each other. Nor are all of our interests the same.

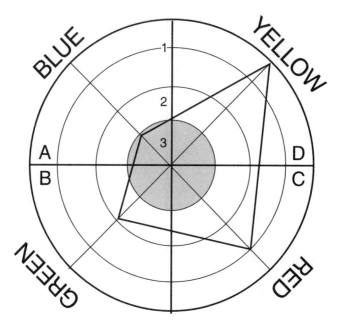

Figure 5.7
HBDI profile for Jim Lewis.

He loves sports—especially soccer—and I am more or less indifferent to them. His political views differ from mine in some instances. He is more strategic in his thinking than I am (the NT Rational being true to form), and I am perhaps more diplomatic in my thinking than he is (the NF Idealist coming through). In spite of these differences, however, we do share an uncanny camaraderie. We "clicked" from our first encounter, being able to communicate almost without words. We feel a bond that is unlike what you feel with people who are very different than yourself.

So, similarity leads to rapport, and rapport is the basis for close personal relationships, for good communication, for feeling that you understand and are being understood, and for cooperation in any endeavor. Lacking rapport, you find it very challenging to deal with another person.

Personality similarities and thinking similarities provide the "common ground" that yields rapport. This is a very important concept for a leader. As I said earlier, Ned Herrmann believed that a square HBDI profile was ideal for a CEO (any leader for that matter) because it would enable the leader to establish that bond, that

Step outside of the box of your own characteristics and meet people "where they live."

rapport, with almost any follower, as the leader could understand and empathize with the thinking of the follower. But what if you don't have a square profile (and the odds are that you don't, since only about 3 percent of the population has this profile)?

The answer is that if you first understand your own temperament and thinking preferences, you can learn to tolerate the differences you encounter, and you can also learn to step outside the box of your own characteristics and meet people "where they live." As a seminar instructor, I have to deal with this all the time. Since my preferred quadrants are C and D, I tend to teach at a very high, conceptual level and emphasize the interpersonal a lot. Those people who prefer to think in quadrants A and B could easily be lost when I do this. They need analysis and detail. They want me to drill down to the "nitty-gritty," instead of staying at the 30,000-foot level. So I have to do this.

I must talk their language. Put another way, I must teach in all four quadrants, and I must teach to all four temperaments. I can't say that I always succeed at doing this, but it is the effort I must make.

What I have found frustrating is that the A and B thinkers don't always understand the concept I am trying to get across.

They are focused on the trees, and I am painting a picture of a forest. Most significantly, they fail to value the C quadrant component—the interpersonal, emotional, humanistic part of the message—and leave me wondering if there is any hope for making the workplace a "kinder, gentler" place to be.

I don't have to worry about the NF temperaments. They are with me. We have instant rapport. They come up during break or after class and tell me how much they enjoyed the class. And the NT Rationals are fairly well served. It is the SJ Guardians whose mismatch is a little stronger for me. But at least we have one thing in common: We are both cooperative in our use of tools, so that provides the basis of overlap.

It is the SP Artisan with whom I would have the greatest degree of mismatch. Remember, they are diagonally opposite me in the matrix, so we are mismatched in communication and tool use. Fortunately for me, most of the Artisans have left the corporate environment, so I don't encounter many of them in seminars on project management.

This would be entirely different for a leader of projects involving the population at large. Here you can expect to have the entire spectrum of temperaments and thinking styles, so you definitely must develop skill in dealing with all of them. Projects such as volunteer services, or those run by social groups, church groups, or political parties can be expected to be more diverse than work groups. But even here, if you look at the mix of temperaments in the entry level of an organization, you will notice that there is a fairly high percentage of Artisans, so if your project teams involve people at that level of the company, you can expect to encounter a broad spectrum as well.

The Law of Requisite Variety

Probably some of you who have read my previous books know that I have written about the law of requisite variety in several of them, and you probably think I am in a rut. So be it. This may be the most important principle of systems for any leader to know, so I make no apology for drilling it into your awareness.

The law of requisite variety says that, in any system of humans or machines, the element in the system with the greatest flexibility in its behavior will control the system. Since the job of the leader is to get a group of people to work together to achieve a goal, that means he or she must have some control of the behavior of the team. Not in the command-and-control sense, however, because that seldom works for a project leader, where the people don't feel that they are compelled to follow orders from a project leader. Furthermore, it isn't leadership if they comply because they feel compelled to do so. It is only leadership if they follow willingly.

The Law of Requisite Variety

In any system of humans or machines, the element in the system with the greatest flexibility in its behavior will control the system.

So what this law says is that you must have more flexibility in your behavior than the variation in behavior presented by the team, or you won't have control. Given that this is true, some of you may already have a sinking feeling. How can you possibly have more flexibility than the composite variety presented by a team? It is hard enough to deal with one person and match his or her behavior, much less that of a dozen people. In fact, it is impossible for any of us to match that much variability. We have all learned certain ways of behaving—I call them patterns—and we fall back on these over and over again.

If you don't quite follow what I am saying, watch your favorite weekly TV program, and just pay attention to one character. Watch that person for several weeks in a row and notice how often they use certain gestures. You may not hear them use the same expressions over and over because the scripts are often written by a variety of authors, but good authors know that they should have their key characters use repetitive phrases to help the reader get a sense of the character's identity. Pay attention to your friends, your colleagues, or your spouse, and you will notice the patterns. Then pay attention to yourself, and you will find the same thing.

These patterns are so strongly ingrained in us that deviating from them feels very uncomfortable, and for some people, it is nearly impossible to do. So how are you going to gain flexibility great enough to deal with a team? You probably won't. You can increase your flexibility, no question about it, but there are limits.

So the answer is to reduce the variation in behavior of the team. This is often attempted by imposing rules and regulations on them, but it never really works unless all of them agree with the rule, in which case it wasn't needed to begin with. Those who disagree will always find a way to circumvent the rule.

The way to reduce variation in a team is through good planning. Every team member is pursuing the common goal, and each has his or her component of the plan to guide individual behavior. When this is true, you don't have to worry about variation so much; it will automatically be minimized, but in a positive way, rather than in the thou-shalt-not negative way.

The First Rule of Planning

The people who must execute the plan should have participated in creating it!

Just one caution. Remember that the only way to get buy-in for a project plan is to follow the first rule of project planning, which says that the people who must execute the plan should have participated in creating it! If you violate this rule, then everything I have said is almost null and void.

Increasing Your Flexibility

I want to be careful here that you don't think all you have to do is good project planning to be effective. You still need as much flexibility as you can muster to be an effective leader because you will constantly be dealing one-on-one with individuals who "think funny," or differ from you in some way.

I think the first step is to develop flexibility in your understanding of people. If you appreciate differences, instead of being threatened by them, then you automatically gain some flexibility. I look at it this way—a different person presents me with the opportunity to learn something. While it is really great to talk with

NO
PLAN
↓
NO
CONTROL

PLANS
are everything!

someone who thinks like I do, I don't learn anything in that situation. I learn when I encounter someone who thinks differently.

In addition, the research on creativity and innovation all shows that you gain the most from diverse teams. In fact, Ned Herrmann did a lot of work on creativity and thinking preferences. Ned was a very talented painter, and he was very interested in the creative process. After many years of experimentation, he concluded that you never get as good task outcomes with single-gender groups as you do with gender-balanced groups. He was a strong advocate for this.

There is, in fact, a slight difference in the population composite profiles for men and women. The composite profile should be square, and for the total population, it comes pretty close. But for men, there is a small "tilt" toward the A quadrant and for women the tilt is toward the C quadrant. That is, men tend to be a bit more analytical than women, and women tend to be a little more interpersonal than men.

In fact, this is the basis of some of the conflicts between men and women—especially in the workplace. Since we tend to have so many executives who are STJs, and very few SFJs, they tend to be put off by the people who attend very much to the C quadrant. These are bleeding hearts to the STJ. If, as we might expect, a female executive happens to be an SFJ, she will probably be seen as too soft on some issues. In addition, the C quadrant is the quadrant of emotion (feeling) so she may be accused of being too emotional.

Nevertheless, what Ned found was that we need the balance in thinking that can only be obtained with a gender-balanced team, so we should strive to create such groups if we want to achieve the best results in projects.

Decision Making in Project Teams

One aspect of this that deserves attention is decision making. Two components affect the effectiveness of decisions made in the workplace. One is the validity of the choice itself, and the other is whether the choice is accepted by everyone affected by it. In the past, validity was called quality, but I have found that this word is too easily confused with other meanings, so perhaps validity is a better choice.

We say that an effective decision is one that has been made in such a way that it is both valid and accepted by everyone affected by it. Validity has to do with either quantitative or qualitative indexes. For example, if you are trying to choose a course of action that has economic impact to the company, which choice is most valid in terms of cost measures? Or if it were a choice of an engineering approach to a problem, you want to choose the one that will perform best, that is, have technical validity. Finally, as another example, you are going for a job interview and you want to dress in such a way that you will make the best impression on the people interviewing you. This one is qualitative, rather than quantitative, but it certainly is a valid concern.

The acceptance dimension is the one most often neglected in organizations, probably because there are so few managers who have strong preferences for thinking in the C quadrant. They make a decision considering only the quantitative or qualitative aspects, but the people affected by it have intense negative reactions to it, and the manager wonders why everyone is being so difficult.

As an example, companies always try to close their fiscal year looking as profitable as possible. To do this, they look for ways to cut expenses near the end of the year. One way to do so is to furlough people for a couple of weeks, without pay. I have had numerous people tell me that their company had them take off two weeks without pay at the end of the year, which had an obviously serious impact on their projects, and then management wondered why the project had slipped two weeks. Go figure.

To the senior manager making this decision, however, it is an economic consideration that drives his or her thinking. If any consideration is given to whether people accept it, that consideration is minimum. But if you could measure the impact to costs of the effect such decisions have on morale, you may very well find that it was greater than the immediate savings of furloughing people.

So what is this all about? It means that when you make an effective decision, you must engage both quadrants A and C. Otherwise, you will have a decision that looks good in terms of validity, but its implementation may be severely impacted because people do not accept it.

In the next chapter, we will examine the specific ways in which leaders must lead in order to be successful.

6

Leadership Styles

The earliest research on leadership attempted to answer the question, "Are leaders born or made?" Or, put differently, do leaders have certain personal attributes that ordinary people don't have? The answer is no. After 50 years of research, the conclusion is that leaders come in all shapes and sizes.

Based on what we have looked at so far, the question may be asked, Is one temperament more effective than another? Or in terms of thinking preferences, Is there a profile that is most effective?

As for temperaments, the answer is not a simple yes or no. It goes more like this: To be effective, the temperament of the leader must either be matched to the requirements of the situation, or the leader must delegate to someone whose temperament does match those requirements if he or she is to be effective over-

Are leaders born or made?

———

Research indicates they are made.

all. We will come back to this in a moment and discuss it in much greater detail.

But what about thinking preferences? We have said that the best profile would be a square one, but since only a few percent of people have such profiles, it would be rare to find a leader who has one. More likely, a leader will have at least a double-dominant profile. Take my profile as an example. Mine is double-dominant in quadrants C and D. My preferred leadership style is going to be high-level, holistic, and interpersonal. But what if the situation calls for some very detailed (quadrant B) work or very analytical (quadrant A) work? Then I either must move into those quadrants when dealing with the team or enlist the help of some other team member to lead the team during that phase of the project.

> *A major task for a leader is to match the proper talent to the requirements of the job.*

Notice again the need for me to be flexible or to delegate to those who have the style needed to deal with the situation. Actually, my job as leader is to *match the proper talent to the requirements of the job.*

Have you ever noticed that a CEO will be highly effective in a company, then get recruited by another organization and wind up getting fired by them? How can this be? If he was effective in one place, why wouldn't he be effective in another?

There are several possibilities. The most likely one is that the situations were different and required different leadership styles. Another is that there were philosophical differences between the new CEO and the board of directors. Either of these may be accounted for by temperament or thinking styles.

For example, suppose the leader is an NT. As we have seen, about 32 percent of CEOs are Rationals. In his previous company, it was the strategic thinking of the NT that was needed to move them through a growth period, and this CEO provided exactly that. So a board of directors, in awe of the CEO's accomplishments, thinks "Maybe he can do that for our company," so they hire him.

However, the first company was young, considerably smaller, and very dynamic. The new company is old, immense, and stable. It is populated mostly with SJ middle managers who do an excellent job of running the company like a clock. But as soon as the new NT CEO tries to change the direction of the company, these very effective middle managers become the obstacle to change. By nature, they resist change. They were "bred" to do so. They are Guardians, keepers of rules and regulations, excellent in handling the logistic needs of the company, and because the organization is successful, they see no reason to change. What is this new guy up to anyway? He's rocking the boat, that's all.

I once saw a beautiful example of this. I was recruited to help a company become more effective. They were in an industry that was experiencing significant threat from Japanese competitors and were trying to survive. So we got the 17 managers together for a weekend retreat and administered the Myers-Briggs to them. It was an amazing finding for me. Sixteen of these managers were SJs, and the fellow who hired me was an NT. Everyone considered him a misfit. He was always rocking the boat. Why couldn't he leave well enough alone? And why did they need to be psychoanalyzed by Jim Lewis? There was nothing wrong with them.

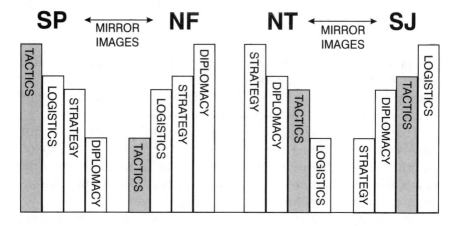

Figure 6.1
Temperament and intelligence.

What this means is that leaders tend to lead in congruence with their dominant intelligence. So, as we have seen from Keirsey, this will involve diplomacy, strategy, tactics, or logistics. I have repeated the figure for your convenience (Figure 6.1).

The SJ leader, then, will prefer to deal with logistics and tactics, while the NT leader will be diametrically opposed, preferring to emphasize strategy and diplomacy. In the case of a company that is in a stable environment, you need the SJ leader's orientation, but in one that is volatile, you may need the NT approach.

CHURCHILL AND GIULIANI

In Chapter 2, I related that after the World Trade Center attacks on September 11, 2001, New York City Mayor Giuliani stayed up all night reading a new biography of Winston Churchill. He probably did so because of the parallels between his situation and the one Churchill faced. Both men found themselves under attack. The Germans were bombing England, and terrorists were attacking the United States.

It is no secret that Winston Churchill was very effective as Prime Minister of England during World War II, but that before and after the war he was not viewed by the people as a leader. It is also no secret that Giuliani was not viewed in very high regard by most New Yorkers on September 10, but a few days later, he was "mayor of the world," to use the *Time* magazine epithet. It remains to be seen if his image will stand the test of time, but my guess is that it will fade, and he, like Churchill, will be remembered as a great "wartime" leader, but not as a perennial one.

Keirsey says that Churchill was an Artisan, a "virtuoso of political maneuvering, wheeling and dealing in unending political skirmishes . . ." (1998, p. 286). He contrasts Churchill with Gandhi, who was an Idealist. These are diametric opposites—the Artisan is the tactician, and the NF is the diplomat. Both did the same thing for their countries—delivered them from bondage—but in totally different ways. Gandhi is famous for his diplomatic approach, advocating nonviolence, the passive response to domination by England, and it worked.

LEADERSHIP IS BEHAVIOR

I have previously said that leadership is not a position, it is behavior. It is influencing others to follow one's lead. I also said that the research showed that it is not personal attributes that make a person a leader. What was found was that different behavior was required for different situations. This led Paul Hersey and Ken Blanchard to formulate a model for leaders to follow, which they called Situational Leadership (1981).

The research showed that there are two important dimensions in a leader's behavior. One is called "task" behavior and the other is called "relationship" behavior. These are portrayed as orthogonal axes in the model Hersey and Blanchard developed. By indicating the "strength" of each dimension simply as high or low, you arrive at four combinations, which can be thought of as four different styles of dealing with a follower. This is shown in Figure 6.2.

To understand this model, begin by considering the dimensions. Directive behavior means that the leader is focused on the task requirements. If his or her behavior is high, it means that a lot of emphasis is being placed on the task itself. Supportive behavior

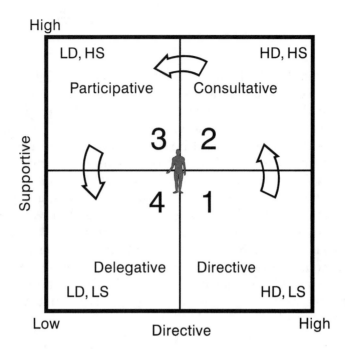

Figure 6.2
Hersey and Blanchard leadership styles.

is an expression of consideration for the follower—offering encouragement, expressing appreciation, and generally letting the follower know that he or she is valued by the leader.

In quadrant one, there is very little supportive behavior expressed. It is mostly a task emphasis. The leadership style for this quadrant is called directive, or sometimes "telling." In quadrant two, there is strong emphasis on the supportive dimension, but there is still a high emphasis on the task itself. This has been called influencing, selling, and consulting by Hersey and Blanchard. In quadrant one, the leader is simply telling the follower what must be done, perhaps how to do it, and by when it must be completed. In quadrant two, however, the leader offers the follower a vote of confidence. The leader may say something like, "Here's what needs to be done, and here is why it should be done this way. You've been doing good work. Keep it up, and let me know if you need anything."

Quadrant three is called participative. There is less emphasis on the task, but still high supportive behavior. The follower is given a great deal more latitude in deciding how a task will be done. The leader may still say what must be done, but not so much how to do it. And finally, quadrant four is delegative. There is low-task (directive) and low-supportive behavior. The follower is simply told what should be done and is then left alone to figure out how to do it.

Now to show why it is important to choose the correct style of leadership, imagine that a company has just hired a young person fresh out of high school. The job is a factory job, running a machine that cost several million dollars. The new employee made a very good impression in the job interview, and her boss is pleased to have her become part of the workforce. She introduces the young lady to the rest of the work group, then shows her the machine she is supposed to run. It is an impressive piece of equipment, with a panel covered with knobs, displays, and switches. The supervisor says, "Here is your machine, Kathy. Your job is to keep this baby running at top capacity. I'll leave it to you to do just that. Good luck." And she walks away.

Of course, this is a quadrant-four, delegative style, and any person who has any intelligence will immediately react by saying, "You made that up! No supervisor could be stupid enough to do that!" I would generally agree, though I have seen supervisors do almost as badly.

What is wrong?

You say, "The new employee should be trained to run the machine. You can't expect her to figure it out by herself. She is going to make a lot of mistakes and probably cost the company a lot of money. Why, she might even get hurt!"

Right on.

The point is that a directive style is called for, and delegative was used. (Actually it is almost more abdication than delegation, but I am stretching the definition a bit to make a point). This reinforces the idea that the correct leadership style is a function of the situation, and the situation is a combination of the job requirements and the skill of the person being assigned to it. In fact, Hersey and Blanchard said that the leader should ask two questions to determine which style is appropriate for the assignment being given to the follower. These questions are:

*Leaders should ask
two questions*

———

*1. Can the person
do the job?*
*2. Will he/she take
responsibility
for it?*

❏ Can the person do the job?
❏ Will he or she take responsibility for it?

If the answer to both questions is no, then you should choose directive as your leadership style. If the answer to both questions is yes, then delegative is in order. All four combinations are shown in the following table.

Can?	Will?	Appropriate Leadership Style
N	N	Directive
N	Y	Consultative
Y	N	Participative
Y	Y	Delegative

Leader Consistency

There is an obvious outcome of this model that some people find contradictory with what they have been taught about leadership. This model says that the appropriate leadership behavior will vary with the assignment a person is given, and most supervisory courses emphasize that a leader should be consistent with followers—not deal with them one way today and a different way tomorrow. This is true where issues of fairness are concerned. You don't impose sanctions on a person for an infraction of a rule today and let her off the hook tomorrow (unless there is a very extenuating circumstance involved). That is a good rule to follow. But we are not talking here about fair treatment, we are talking about how you deal with the person in terms of task assignments. And we are saying that when the person has very little experience with a task, she needs a lot more direction than when she is more experienced.

I have found in my 20 years of dealing with this model that managers tend to have some trouble with quadrants one and four. They often are not directive enough when it is required, opting instead for quadrant two, which isn't strong enough in some cases. Perhaps it is an aversion that they themselves have for being told what to do. I'm not sure, but I do know that some managers have problems being properly directive.

Many of them also have trouble delegating. The reason for this is simple: Answering the two questions, *can* and *will*, is difficult for them. They aren't sure the person can do the job or will take responsibility for it, and if the follower drops the ball, the manager is in trouble. So rather than take that risk, they will use a participative style, which is a little too heavy for a person who is truly competent and who would take the job and run with it, given the chance.

Delegating involves some risk-taking the first time you give a person a certain assignment. It is true, you may not be sure if she can handle it. But you will never find out unless you take a chance. That is the catch. I often use the example of having your teenage daughter get a driver's license. You know that when she comes home, she wants to drive the car—solo, of course. And there is only one thing you can do—give her the keys and hope she doesn't have an accident. If you don't take the chance, you will be driving her around until she is 40 years old, and that won't be any fun for either of you!

Situational Leadership and Thinking Styles

I believe that the leaders who will have the most difficulty with situational leadership are those who have very low scores in the C quadrant. They do not think interpersonally, or emotionally. They may well find it difficult to express caring feelings. In terms of temperaments, the STJ and SPJ individuals will fall into this category. The NFs won't have as much trouble, although there is a gender difference. In our society, we have the idea that men don't express "tender" feelings for others, except maybe their spouses. So we find that many men can express anger, criticism, and other negative emotions, but will only give people "strokes" under rare circumstances. This is a problem. You will remember that Keirsey has said part of the leader's job is to express appreciation to followers for their contributions, and that those who make the greatest contribution have the greatest need for expressions of appreciation. Thus, there are two factors at work here that create some difficulties for being a good leader: one's own temperament and the conditioning of society.

Applying Situational Leadership to the Project Team

The way a project leader launches a project can make or break him. A project is a problem to be solved, and when people are faced with solving a problem, they look to someone in the team to help give them some direction, to provide a structured approach that they feel confident will help them achieve the goal.

I once saw a group begin solving a problem in a classroom, and one member said, "Oh, I've seen this before." Immediately the group started looking to him for help in solving the problem. The only thing is, he may have seen it before, but he couldn't remember how to solve it, so within minutes, the group turned to another person who seemed to have a good approach, and he became their leader.

In terms of the situational leadership model, this means that the leader needs to start in quadrant one, or possibly two, with a new project team. Tell them what is going to be done. Tell them how

The way a project leader launches a project can make or break him.

the project planning will be done. Notice you aren't telling them how the problem will be solved, but you are telling them how the problem solving will be approached. This is the kind of structure they need to get themselves organized.

You also need to do what Giuliani and Churchill did: express confidence that the goal can be reached. You must be optimistic, supportive, in charge. People don't want to follow a wimp. If you seem uncertain, fearful, or hesitant, they will all be scared to death to be members of your team.

Perhaps this is more quadrant two than quadrant one because you are doing some obvious "selling." That is probably appropriate for a team, in that you seldom have a project team that is in quadrant one in terms of their job maturity. You ask if they can do the job. If not, why do you have this particular team? Why not go get another one? You ask if they will take responsibility for the work. I expect that most of them will. Some may need a little more hand-holding and pep talk than others, but for the most part the answer should be yes. So you may only need to get into quadrant one with your team in rare circumstances when they have hit a real snag.

FUNDAMENTAL INTERPERSONAL RELATIONS ORIENTATION (FIRO)

Will Schutz has written that in dealing with other people each of us has preferences for behavior in three areas. He called these *inclusion, control,* and *affection.* Inclusion means being included in activities with others. Control has to do with who makes decisions, who "calls the shots," and who has influence. Affection means expressions of liking for each other, for caring, and for love in those relations for which love is appropriate.

Because these behaviors can be both expressed and received, he said that for each of us there is a degree of how much inclusion we like to express toward others and how much we want them to express toward us. The same is true for the other two behaviors. Schutz developed an instrument to measure the strength of one's wanted and expressed inclusion, wanted and expressed control, and wanted and expressed affection.

Inclusion Concerns

What do you suppose is one of the first concerns of members of a new team? Inclusion, of course. Each person wants to know whether the other team members view her as a valuable team member. She wants to know what role she will be expected to play and whether she will be able to meet those requirements. She also wants to find out if membership in this team is something she will really find rewarding—in other words, does she really want to belong to this group?

A team leader has another task to perform in a new team, then: addressing the inclusion concerns of all members. They should be introduced to each other (unless you are very sure that they already know each other pretty well), and their expected contribution to team performance should be stated to all of the group. It helps to say that you are glad to have each person as a member, that you are confident they will be able to work well together, and that you are there to help them.

Since individuals differ in the amount of inclusion they want, some of them won't be very keen on being in a team—they would rather work alone. You shouldn't expect these people to be what we usually call real team players, but if you are in a situation where they can do most of their work on their own, then this is not a problem. On the other hand, if you need close collaboration among members of the team, then you really need members whose wanted inclusion scores are at least moderately high.

This is one reason why, if you have a choice, the best way to form a project team is to solicit volunteers. Since that is not always possible, you have to settle for the next best thing, which is the ability to eject those who don't fit. That should not be considered a black mark against them either; it is just a personal characteristic that makes them a poor candidate for certain kinds of jobs. They will do fine in other situations.

Control Concerns

As the team begins working in earnest, the next concern to emerge is control. Members want to know if the leader is really in charge. Are they headed in the right direction? Who is going to make decisions? How much input will each member have?

If you as leader fail to address these concerns, you may find the team playing "get the leader." They will try to unseat you. You must hold the mission and vision of the project in front of them and assure them that the goal is clear and that they are headed in the right direction. You must also assure them that decisions will be handled at the appropriate level and in the appropriate way. Some will be autonomous; others will be by consensus.

Affection Concerns

This is where expressions of appreciation for contributions becomes important. If you fail to do this, you will be seen as uncaring and unappreciative. Again, since each person has a differing strength of need for such expressions, you have to gauge each person separately. Don't worry, each person will let you know. You can always tell when a person has high approval needs. But don't be misled by signs of slight embarrassment when you "stroke"

Members want to know if the leader is really in charge.

———

Are they headed in the right direction?

some individuals. You will be tempted to think that these people don't want strokes, but that may not be the case. It is just that some are a little embarrassed when you compliment them. This tends to be true more for introverts than extroverts, and since about 75 percent of engineers, programmers, and other technical people are introverts, it applies to them.

Technical people have very high appreciation needs, but they really are insistent that it be genuine, and the dilemma for a leader is that they are suspicious of anyone complimenting them if that person does not understand their work. This is another reason why technical people are best led by a person who has a technical education.

Team Development and Leadership Styles

I doubt that many of you reading this book are unaware of the team development phases called *forming, storming, norming,* and *performing.* These terms were first written about by Bruce Tuckman (1965). In the forming stage, members of the team are very concerned about inclusion, as I said above. In the storming

STAGE	THEME	TASK OUTCOME	RELATIONSHIP OUTCOME
Forming	Awareness	Commitment	Acceptance
Storming	Conflict	Clarification	Belonging
Norming	Cooperation	Involvement	Support
Performing	Productivity	Achievement	Pride

Table 6.1
Task and relationship outcomes for each stage of team development.

stage, they are concerned about control. As they reach the norming phase, concerns about control begin to give way to concerns about affection, and these probably reach their full bloom in the performing phase.

The concerns of each phase are shown in Table 6.1. Note that it also shows the task and relationship outcomes that must be achieved if the team is to reach maturity. (This table is adapted from Kormanski and Mozenter, 1987.)

Kormanski and Mozenter went on to say that the appropriate leadership style for each phase is provided by the situational leadership model, so that forming corresponds to the directive style, storming requires the consultative style, norming is best managed through participative approaches, and performing corresponds to the delegative style.

There is a very strong tendency to want to get past the storming phase as fast as possible, before everyone gets beaten up too badly. This is a mistake. If you bypass this phase without addressing the issues, the team will simply keep revisiting it, and your progress will be impeded. It is really best to get it out into the open and deal with it. Notice that members of the team want clarification of their mission and assurance that they are accepted as valuable members of the team. Effective leaders must take positive steps to assure them that they are on the right track and that they are valued, as I said previously. If you don't do this, you will probably suffer some casualties, as some members will bail out if they have the option.

TO SUMMARIZE

No single style of leadership is best. The appropriate style depends on the situation, which means the ability and willingness of the follower to perform a given task. Furthermore, since the ability and willingness of the entire team varies as the team develops, the leadership style appropriate for each phase of team development follows the situational leadership model.

In the next chapter, we will examine what leaders actually do.

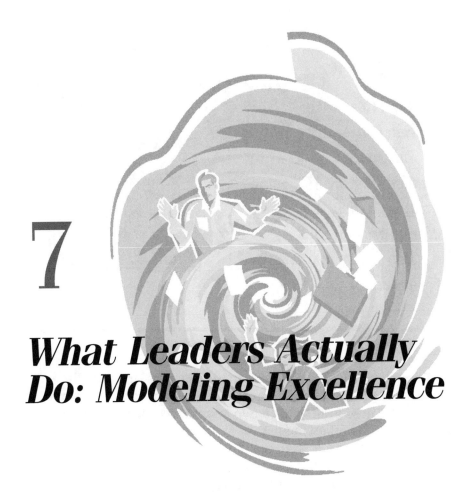

7

What Leaders Actually Do: Modeling Excellence

T he best way to learn how to do something really well is to find someone who is already proficient at the behavior and imitate him or her. This is exactly what Kouzes and Posner did in 1985. They surveyed leaders and asked a simple question: "When you are leading people and it is working, what are you doing?" From this survey, they found several common practices that leaders reported following when they were effective. They called these VIP, which stands for vision, involvement, and persistence.

Effective leaders first establish a clear *vision* of where they are going, and get others to buy into it. They do this by *involving* them in the task, so that they feel ownership for it. And last, they are *persistent* in their pursuit of that vision, in spite of setbacks and difficulties.

Effective leaders are always challenging the way in which things are done (that is the process).

To make more explicit how these practices are actually executed, Kouzes and Posner broke them down into five smaller "chunks." These in turn have two subpractices for each category, as shown in the following list.

LEADERSHIP PRACTICES

Challenging the Process

Effective leaders are never satisfied with the status quo. They are always challenging the way in which things are done, that is, the process. Put simply, good leaders are always looking for a better way. Since this is a characteristic of NT leaders but not of SJ individuals, we might ask if this means the Guardian is by definition an ineffective leader. The answer is a resounding no!

All of the temperaments can be effective leaders. What it does mean is that the SJ leader must set aside his or her tendency to be a stabilizer, to live by the motto, "If it ain't broke, don't fix it," and to instead adopt the motto, "If it ain't broke, break it and then fix it." Furthermore, the SJ leader must take risks by trying unproven approaches. Since corporate America is largely risk-averse, the SJ

Kouzes & Posner's
Leadership Practices

Challenging the process
1. Search for opportunities
2. Experiment and take risks

Inspiring a shared vision
3. Envision the future
4. Enlist others

Enabling others to act
5. Foster collaboration
6. Strengthen others

Modeling the way
7. Set the example
8. Plan small wins

Encouraging the heart
9. Recognize individual contribution
10. Celebrate accomplishments

---

leader must fight this tendency. I believe that those with the SJ temperament may find this the hardest practice to engage in, but I believe they can do it.

Inspiring a Shared Vision

I would be so bold as to say that a leader without vision is a leader without followers. People only get excited about inspiring vision. In fact, Warren Bennis has written a book entitled *Managing the Dream* (2000), in which he says that this is what differentiates great leaders from those who are only followers: They are able to communicate to their followers a vision of the future that inspires them to sacrifice, to work really hard, and to sometimes give up their personal interests in pursuit of the leader's vision.

I would argue that this is the explanation for all of the world's great monuments, both ancient and modern. When the World Trade Center was demolished by terrorists, it was a blow to Americans everywhere because the trade center buildings represented something great. It was a triumph of human ingenuity, engineering, and spirit to erect buildings that tall, and for someone to deliberately destroy them was an affront to the American character.

In the same way, the great cathedrals, the Mayan pyramids, the Egyptian pyramids, Stonehenge, the Eiffel tower, and many other structures were built at great expense of human effort and money. Why? Because the people who built them had a dream. The stones used to build Stonehenge are found only in a site 100 or more miles away and had to be transported over that great distance through considerable effort. Then the stones had to be shaped and placed upright. You don't do this for fun, nor can you explain it as the byproduct of slave labor.

In my book *Working Together,* which is an exposition on the management principles espoused by Alan Mulally, President and CEO of Boeing Commercial Airplanes, I explain that his first principle is to begin with a compelling vision. A compelling vision, not some watered-down, ho-hum idea that excites no one. Perhaps a good example is the vision of every athlete—especially prizefighters. Each wants to be the "greatest," the champion. It isn't enough to be second or third. Teams and individuals want to be number one, and they will go to great effort to become champions. It is that vision of being number one that drives them.

Mulally inspired a team of over 2,100 engineers with his vision for the 777 airplane by creating a small button that carried the expression, *Denver to Honolulu on a hot day.* Walt Gillette, who was chief project engineer for airplane performance, safety, and reliability on the 777 program, wrote me and explained that "Denver to Honolulu on a hot day" meant all of the following:

❑ *It was very visual—in our mind's eye, we could imagine ourselves as the captain and first officer of this flight, seeing the heat
   waves rising off the concrete runway in the thin air of Denver,
   and having full confidence that our silver machine would take us
   safely into the air.*

❑ *"Denver" meant that the airplane had the high altitude capability
   from the onset to do this difficult mission.*

❑ *"Hot day" meant that the airplane had gone into revenue service
   in the summer, as promised five years earlier.*

❑ *"Honolulu" meant that the airplane had ETOPS ability at the
   start of revenue service.*

    *These images in the minds of the 777 creation team evoked by
"Denver to Honolulu on a hot day" spoke to the heart in a way
that facts and data could not. Each of us was able to internalize
what our share of the assignment meant to achieving this vision.*
(Personal correspondence. Used by permission.)

Mulally's button is shown in Figure 7.1. The airplane is a car-
toon that Mulally is fond of drawing. It is a simple thing, yet it
conveyed an image that drove the team to produce what many pilots and technologists consider to be the world's greatest airplane.

Enabling Others to Act

This principle says that an effective leader fosters collaboration
and strengthens others. Good leaders are facilitators. They make it
easier for people to do their jobs, not harder.

    Unfortunately, the law of requisite variety is an enemy of en-
abling others. The reason is that managers intuitively sense that
they must reduce the variation in behavior of people in their organizations, or they will lose control. So they pass all sorts of
rules and regulations about what people cannot do. These are
called *company policy,* and policy manuals are often several
inches thick or even several volumes in size. Ostensibly, they are
touted as a mechanism to improve decision-making efficiency.
By establishing a policy, managers don't have to make the same
decisions over and over. The problem is, who can remember a
thousand policies? Once you exceed about 10 policies, you exceed

Figure 7.1
Mulally's 777 button.

the ability of people to remember them, and the effectiveness theory goes out the window.

Besides, as I wrote in Chapter 2, the only people who obey policies are those who agree with them. Those who disagree find ways to circumvent them. The only thing the policy manual does for a company is get them off the hook in case an employee violates the rule and is sanctioned and then tries to sue the company. So long as there was a written policy forbidding the sanctioned behavior, the company is blameless.

Those "thou-shalt-not" policies are just too much for Artisans, so they tend to get out of the corporate world and do their own thing. Remember, they are utilitarian in their use of tools, which means that they do whatever works to get the job done, and they find prescriptions to be too confining. They also abhor deadlines and regimen. These confine their flexibility, their desire to keep their options open.

The SJ guardians, who are 60 percent of all senior managers, are schedule- and regimen-driven, and so the poor SP is immediately oppressed by the SJ approach to managing. He or she feels disabled, rather than enabled.

There is an interesting paradox here. The SJ is extremely good at logistics, remember, and it is the tools, equipment, supplies, and so on that enable people to get their jobs done. If it weren't for the attention given these issues by the SJ managers, most organizations might quickly grind to a halt. The negative is that the same SJ who provides the materiel will also place obstacles in the way of using them. They must be used in prescribed ways, not wasted, and so on. Again, this is because the SJ is cooperative in the use of tools and thinks it is shameful to misuse materiel.

This principle essentially advocates empowering employees. This is a touchy subject and one that is much misunderstood. Many managers believe it means that the business is turned over to employees to run and that managers can no longer direct them. This is ludicrous. But it was expressed very well by the CEO of a large corporation that went under. "I'm not going to let the monkeys run the business," he said.

Of course, this comment conveys a strong disdain for his workers, and is (in my opinion) a good sign of why his company ultimately died. But it also conveys a misunderstanding of empowerment. You do not turn the company over to the employees to run, but you do make it possible for them to do their jobs with minimum direction and interference from managers. To do so, you must create conditions where delegation is possible. This means that you must be able to answer an emphatic YES to the questions, Can they do the job? and Will they take responsibility for it? You will only be able to answer affirmatively if you have properly trained your people, given them adequate information, helped them plan the job properly, and given them a clear definition of their authority to act unilaterally.

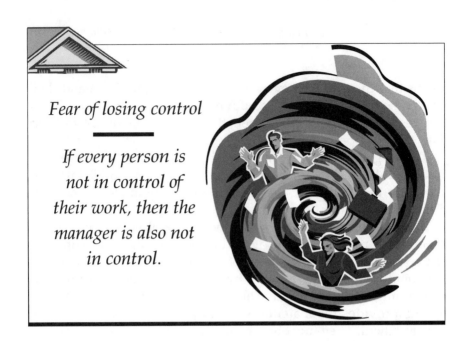

Fear of losing control

If every person is not in control of their work, then the manager is also not in control.

Fear of Losing Control

I believe that a major reason so many managers are afraid to delegate and empower their followers is that they fear losing control. What they don't realize is that, if every person is not in control of his or her work, then the manager is also not in control. That is, you must make it possible for individuals to be in control of their own work if you are to be in control yourself. If you don't believe this, just consider what happens if one worker on your project critical path gets off track. The project starts slipping. It makes no difference that everyone else is on schedule, this person is going to sink your schedule. So you won't have control unless everyone is in control.

Modeling the Way

We have all heard it said that leaders have to "walk the talk" if they are to be respected by followers. It also is unsaid but true that if followers don't respect leaders, they quit following them, so we can surmise that leaders who don't walk the talk wind up with no followers.

This is called setting the example. When the Trade Center towers were on fire and collapsing, Giuliani put himself at some risk by

L-E-A-D
by example

Leaders have to
"walk the talk"
if they are to be
respected by
followers.

going to the scene to assist. Many of the firefighters who died perished with their leaders. These men and women know the need to lead by example, to live by the credo that they never expect their followers to do anything that they themselves wouldn't do.

But modeling the way is an extremely broad thing. It not only includes behavior but character as well. No one respects the leader who is dishonest, who lies, who cheats, or who breaks the law. A leader can't get by with telling people to "Do as I say, not as I do." He or she must be better than that. In fact, we almost expect our leaders to be even better than we are.

As I write this, the Catholic church is undergoing a crisis of confidence. A number of their priests have admitted to molesting children, and it has been disclosed that these offenses were known to cardinals and bishops who did nothing about them. This has provoked a real sense of foul play among devout Catholics. Clergy should be beyond reproach. They should be sinless, for don't they stand in the pulpit every Sunday and admonish their flock to abstain from sin?

In addition, the second component of modeling the way is for the leader to plan small wins for followers. This is an extremely important idea. Nothing destroys confidence quicker than immediate failure at something. I learned this years ago when I taught guitar. Most methods started beginners with learning the chords C, F, and G7. The problem is that the F chord is almost impossible for a beginner to make initially. It requires strength and finger coordination that they simply don't yet have. So after a week of struggling with the F chord, the student returns looking downcast, and says, "I don't think I'll ever be able to make the F chord."

I quickly realized that this was a bad start. They were having a failure experience rather than a success experience. So I switched to a new set of chords that were much easier, and the following week the students were proud—these were chords they could make! Then, progressively, they learned to make the harder chords.

The other thing I learned was that music students become learners because they want to emulate some master that they have heard. In the case of guitar, it could be Segovia. So they want to be able to play like Segovia by the end of the week, and of course, that isn't possible. But what do we do? We have them start learning scales! My gosh, there is nothing musical about scales. It is far better to teach them a simple piece, so they feel successful. Then you can tell them the value of learning scales. "If you practice scales it will help you play this piece even better," you say, and they believe you by this time. Given nothing but scales to play, many lose interest and quit.

Encouraging the Heart

Well, here we are back to what Keirsey said about appreciating contributions. Kouzes and Posner found that this was absolutely correct; you must recognize individual contributions. And you must celebrate team accomplishments. As I have already written, all too often a team achieves an objective at great sacrifice, and management passes over it like it was just routine. The net result is that people feel very unappreciated and move to another job where someone just might value what they contribute. Since I have commented on this at length, I simply submit that research bears out the need for this practice.

Celebrate team accomplishments

When a team achieves its objective, don't treat it as "just routine."

THE "I" VERSUS "WE" LEADER

Another aspect of what leaders actually do was discovered by David McClelland (1975). He read transcripts or listened to speeches given by leaders and found that those judged effective by most people differed from ineffective leaders in their use of language. Specifically, those leaders who were judged effective talked about how "we" will succeed, whereas those judged ineffective used the expression, "I" want to do this. It was *our* objectives as opposed to *my* objectives.

Churchill was a good example. In his first speech as prime minister, given May 13, 1940, to the House of Commons, Churchill said,

> *We have before us an ordeal of the most grievous kind. We have before us many, many long months of struggle and of suffering. You ask, what is our policy? I can say: It is to wage war, by sea, land and air, with all our might and with all the strength that God can give us; to wage war against a monstrous tyranny, never surpassed in the dark, lamentable catalogue of human crime. That is our policy. You ask, what is our aim? I can answer in one word: It is victory, victory at all costs, victory in spite of all terror, victory, however long and hard the road may be; for without victory, there*

is no survival. Let that be realized; no survival for the British Empire, no survival for all that the British Empire has stood for, no survival for the urge and impulse of the ages, that mankind will move forward towards its goal. But I take up my task with buoyancy and hope. I feel sure that our cause will not be suffered to fail among men. At this time I feel entitled to claim the aid of all, and I say, "come then, let us go forward together with our united strength." (http://www.winstonchurchill.org/blood.htm)

As you can see, Churchill appeals to the "we" motive. Together we will be victorious. In fact, as part of this speech, he uttered his famous line, "I would say to the House, as I said to those who have joined this government: 'I have nothing to offer but blood, toil, tears and sweat.'" In this comment, he casts himself as the servant of the people, a title he used to describe himself when, after the war ended, the British people voted him out of office in a landslide for the opposition. But Churchill was not vindictive. He said simply that the British people had suffered much. When the king offered him a knighthood, he declined, saying that he could not accept the honor when the people had given him the boot.

8

The Self-Fulfilling Prophecy and Leadership

A*s a leader,* your job is to get people to do what needs to be done, but this also implies that you want to get them to perform at a high level. In Chapter 3 I said that Peter Drucker wrote that a manager must get people to go beyond minimum acceptable performance in the job, because that level is survival, and an organization must do more than survive—it must improve itself. As Dr. Deming once said, there are two kinds of organizations, those that are getting better and those that are dying. If you are standing still, you're dying—you just don't know it yet (1986).

Now let's consider the self-fulfilling prophecy and what it means for achieving this outcome. The self-fulfilling prophecy says that you get from people what you expect of them. So if you expect high performance, you get it, and vice versa. Certainly they won't ever perform at a level greater than their capability, but unless you

Leaders get people to do what needs to be done, and to perform at a high level.

expect that level of performance from them, you won't even achieve the level they are capable of.

Remember my comments about the difficulty some managers have in delegating, because they are not sure the person can do the job or will take responsibility for it? What do you suppose you communicate to the employee in that case? Certainly not that you have high confidence in him or her. You are showing the opposite by giving more instruction than you would if you were delegating. You are unconsciously signaling your doubts, your fears, or your concerns about the person's ability.

In that case, the person may give you more than you expect, in an attempt to prove that she is capable, but if you continue to convey doubts to her, over time she is likely to shrug her shoulders and say, "What's the use? This manager is clueless. There's no use in working hard, because he doesn't get it anyway." So, in time, you get from her what you expected—less-than-optimal work.

On the other hand, suppose you have just hired a person you believe to be a star performer. You express confidence in her, you spend a lot of time coaching her, showing her the ropes, sharing with her your own knowledge of the job. And guess what happens: She performs like the star you believed her to be.

Some managers have difficulty delegating because they are not sure the person can do the job.

Now you may say that she was a star and your behavior had nothing to do with it. Don't you believe it! Suppose she was actually hired by two managers, one who believed she would be a star and one who had a less-optimistic view of her. She does work for both managers over time. You can bet that her work for the manager who thinks she is a star will be better than the work she does for the other manager.

JAIME ESCALANTE REVISITED

In my story about Jaime Escalante teaching math, you will remember that when he wanted to teach calculus to his students, the head of the math department protested that these were fragile children, and that if he pushed them too hard, he could destroy their confidence. His response was, "They will rise to the level of our expectations of them."

What he was saying had been demonstrated by Rosenthal and Jacobsen years ago in schools. They administered aptitude tests to children, then paired those with the same level of aptitude. They then randomly selected one of them to be an "average" kid. The other was labeled a "late bloomer." Then, without telling the teacher the actual scores for the children, they simply said that one child was average and the other was a late bloomer. The late bloomers were expected to make great strides forward that year, to achieve academic performance far beyond what might normally be expected.

At the end of the year they then looked at the grades these children had received, and sure enough, the late bloomers were doing significantly better than the "average" children, which meant that the teachers had brought about the expected result, since, with them being paired in terms of aptitude scores, there really should have been no difference in their performance.

In another experiment the researchers asked how this mechanism worked. They created the same expectation about late bloomers versus average kids for a different group and different teachers, and they then observed classroom interactions through a one-way mirror, so that the experimenters could not be seen by the students or teacher. What they found was striking. The teachers attended to their late bloomers differently than their average kids. They gave them more leeway, coached them more, and encouraged them more than they did the "average" kids. In doing so, they brought about the expected performance.

When you think about it, there is a really important implication for teachers and managers in this mechanism. Teachers and managers both want to see their followers perform well, and they are rewarded when this happens. Behavior that is rewarded tends to be repeated, so the better the student or employee performs, the better the teacher and manager feel, and the more attention they give the follower, hoping for even better performance. This is called a positive feedback loop, which reinforces itself.

When the student or employee does not perform at an exceptional level, however, the leader is not rewarded (encouraged) and feels no inclination to spend much time with the follower. As some have said, "Why spend time with the kids who show no promise?" This is a negative feedback loop, which either stabilizes or extinguishes the interaction altogether.

Of course, when you think about it, just the opposite should happen. That is, the teacher should spend time coaching the average child even more than would be normal, and in doing so, the child could be expected to perform even better. Jaime Escalante proved this with his kids, who, you will remember, called him quimo—a teacher who teaches dumb kids. And in working so hard with his kids, Escalante got performance out of them that no one ever expected could be achieved.

This does not mean, of course, that the good kids should be ignored. No way. When they are coached and encouraged, you can expect that they will perform even better. So what we really are saying is that leaders can get a lot more out of their followers than they ever dreamed, if they are willing to invest the effort required.

AN EXAMPLE FROM WORK

I have a friend (I'll call him Pete) who manages a very large group of programmers, and when he took over this group, there was one woman who took an immediate dislike to him. Perhaps because she disliked him, she also did not perform her work very well.

The natural tendency would be for Pete to avoid her, because he sensed that she didn't like him. But he did the opposite. He spent more time with her. He coached her. He talked with her about her assignments and tried to ensure that she was matched properly to them so that she was capable of doing the work. He encouraged her and complimented her on her good work. Soon she became a good performer, and the animosity she felt for him vanished. I know this to be true because she told me herself that she initially disliked Pete, but that after she got to know him, he turned out to be OK.

A less-skilled manager, or one unwilling to spend the time with her, would probably have wound up firing her, because over time the dislike she felt for him would have been reciprocated, and it would eventually have escalated into a full-blown conflict. Pete, however, sees such situations as a challenge, and he enjoys seeing if he can "win" in such instances. He doesn't always, but he wins more than he loses.

We tend to get from people what we expect from them. But skilled managers often turn negatives into win-win situations.

WHAT DO YOU BELIEVE?

Since we tend to get from people what we expect of them, and what we expect is a function of what we believe about people, it is important that we examine our beliefs. All of us have beliefs about what the world is like, which includes the people in it. These are called paradigms, or models of reality. The importance of paradigms lies in the fact that we behave consistently with them, but there is a catch. We don't always consciously know what we really believe.

Chris Argyris (1990) has called this the difference between our theory-espoused and our theory-in-use. What we *say* we believe is our theory-espoused. What we really believe (though we are not aware of it) is our theory-in-use, and it is the true belief that governs our behavior.

As an example of this, I once worked with a small group and had them do a consensus exercise. There was only one woman in the group. They were seated around a circular table, and the fellow who emerged as leader was polling the group to see what each member thought about an issue. To my surprise, he skipped over the woman. I stopped them and said, "Do you know what you just did?" No they didn't. I said, "You passed over Marie." They were all surprised. "Yes, you did," said Marie.

I am sure if I had asked them if they were prejudiced against women, they would all have denied it. But their behavior spoke louder than their words would have. And I have seen similar prejudice many times in teams where the person facilitating would ignore people that he didn't like, or about whom he felt some prejudice. I suspect that these facilitators are unaware of their prejudice in many cases, but it is there.

So exactly what do you believe about people when it comes to the workplace? Here are some questions to help you think about this:

1. Do you think most people want to do a good job?
2. Do you believe most people are motivated by pay or the work itself?
3. Do you trust most people to keep on working even if you aren't around?
4. Do you think most people are pretty "straight" with you, or that most of them have hidden agendas that they are trying to advance?
5. Do you believe that you must protect yourself from political maneuvering by other would-be managers?
6. Do you think people will take advantage of you if they get a chance?
7. Do you think you can depend on most workers to do what they say they will do?

Now look at your answers. Is your view of people largely positive or negative? If it is largely negative, then I predict that you will find exactly what you believe to be true. There is a story that illustrates this.

A man moved from one town to another. Shortly after he arrived in the new town, he asked a man, "What kind of people live here?"

Before answering, the man said, "Well, what kind of people lived in the town you came from?"

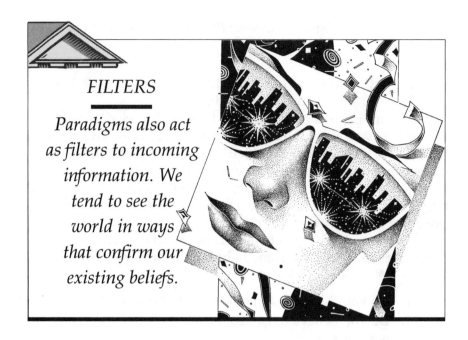

FILTERS

Paradigms also act as filters to incoming information. We tend to see the world in ways that confirm our existing beliefs.

"Oh, they were pretty bad," said the man. "That's why I left. They were mean, nasty, and unfriendly."

"Well, I hate to tell you," said the man, "But that's what you're going to find here."

FILTERS

Paradigms not only reflect what we believe about the world and govern our behavior, but they also act as filters to incoming information. We tend to see the world in ways that confirm our existing beliefs. So if we believe most people are mean, nasty, and unfriendly, then we will see most of them that way, regardless of whether they "objectively" are that way.

The way such filtering works is through deletion and distortion of incoming information. We tend to delete information that would dis-confirm a belief. We don't even notice such evidence. And if we are made aware of it, we interpret it in such a way that we can maintain our belief. This is distortion.

An example of both processes at work came from a marriage counseling session, in which a man complained that his wife never demonstrated that she cared for him. (I suspect he had a high need to receive expressions of affection.) The counselor observed over several sessions that this was not true, that the man's wife did express affection for him. So he asked if the man had noticed these gestures, and he had not. Now, however, once made aware that something was going on about which he was unaware, he admitted the possibility but said, "Oh, she's just doing that for your benefit." First he was deleting the information from his perception, but when made aware of it, he changed its meaning, so he could continue to believe that she was undemonstrative.

WHERE MODELS COME FROM

The question is, why would each of us have general beliefs about what people are like? And the answer is, of course, that they are formed early in life. If, for example, a child goes into school and for some reason is perceived different than the other kids, they may poke fun at him, tease him, and make him miserable. I saw this when I was a child with children who came from poor families. They wore clothing typical of poor children and were teased for it.

We could expect that some of these children would conclude that other kids aren't very nice, and that this belief might generalize to adults as they grow up. In other words, a few bad experiences and a person concludes that the world is not a very nice place.

WHAT TO DO IF YOU HAVE A NEGATIVE VIEW OF PEOPLE

The first inclination would be to say you shouldn't be a manager. But you don't have to live with a worldview forever. It can be changed. The question is how.

I must admit that it isn't easy, but here is an approach that I have found helpful. First let me present you with some beliefs I have about the nature of human beings. I don't claim that these are true, but I have found them helpful. Certainly they may not be true for every person, but perhaps they are generally true, which is what matters. The question is, why do people behave as they do? Here are my answers:

- All behavior is an attempt to satisfy the needs of the individual.
- Because the individual may have learned only one behavior that has worked in the past, he or she can be said to be making the best or only choice available for satisfying the given need.
- The individual is not his or her behavior! We tend to label people "bad, mad, or crazy" because of the negative impact of their behavior, but the person is no more his or her behavior than a computer is its programs.
- All behavior makes sense from the perspective of the actor. The only reason it seems inexplicable to us is that we do not share that person's perspective.
- People have beliefs about what the world is like, which are called models of reality, and they tend to behave consistently with those beliefs.
- People preserve their models through deletion and distortion.

SATISFYING NEEDS

At the very basic level, all behavior is an attempt to satisfy the needs of the individual. Since there is a very wide range of human needs, we may not be able to easily understand the need someone is trying to satisfy, but you can bet it is there.

MAKING THE BEST CHOICE

A person's behavior can sometimes seem bizarre, and we may wonder why anyone would behave that way. Some actions, for example, are totally self-defeating, and we wonder why the person can't see what she is doing to herself.

What is interesting is that she may be aware that her behavior is self-destructive, and tell you that she can't help herself. You see this all the time on some of the more bizarre talk shows. Some of the guests are really strange, but we have to give them some sympathy because they truly feel unable to do anything differently.

This is usually because they have learned only one way to satisfy some need, and they have no flexibility to behave in a different manner.

BACK TO LEADERSHIP

I'm afraid a project manager with a fairly negative view of people is in trouble. A general manager is in enough trouble with a negative view, but it is going to be even worse for a project manager. I would expect that a department manager who has a negative view is going to rule his or her people with an iron hand. They will be closely supervised. They will have very little latitude. Most likely, they will have to get approval from their boss to do almost anything.

Now let that same manager become a project manager, where the people in the project team don't belong to him, and guess what happens. He is going to be wondering all the time if they are doing a good job because he can't closely supervise or control them. My guess is that he may make functional managers—who the people actually report to—miserable by constantly checking up on everyone.

The upshot of all this is that as a leader you must have high expectations for people, or you will get less from them. In addition, if you have high expectations and they "deliver" what you expect, remember that they will want a lot of appreciation. This is how you create that positive feedback loop with them, and this is actually what you want to do. Plan small wins. Encourage them. Be sure they share your vision for the final outcome of their work. And let them know you appreciate their work, rather than just expecting them to do it because they are being paid.

A WORD OF CAUTION ABOUT TEMPERAMENTS

The concern I have about using temperaments to understand people is that it is easy to fall into stereotyping. You begin to believe that if a person is an SJ, then by golly, they are like this and that and the other, and you can really be off in your categorization. Part of the reason is that most people are not pure S or pure J. They have some N in their profile, and some T, so they share characteristics with the NT temperament. The other reason—and the most important—is that the Myers-Briggs only measures four dimensions of personality, and there are no doubt many more that affect the specific way in which a person behaves. The best you can say for temperaments is that they provide you with an idea of the *tendencies* you can expect to find in a person. From there, you must begin differentiating.

9

Communication and Leadership

T here is a (not very serious) theory of leadership called the "big mouth" theory, which suggests that those individuals who talk the most in a group emerge as leader. It is a partial truth. It would be more accurate to say that those individuals who have high ability to express themselves become leaders. Winston Churchill was considered to be the consummate speech maker. As one writer put it:

> *Although he claimed, "I have nothing to offer but blood, toil, tears and sweat," these qualities do not quite fully explain how Sir Winston Churchill helped lead the Allied Powers to victory in World War II. To this list, the word speech should be added, for it was through Churchill's oratories that much of the war was won.*
> (Jonathan Lohn, unpublished article; used by permission.)

Interestingly, on the other side of the war, it was the speech making of Adolph Hitler that may well have accounted for his rise to power because there can be no doubt that his speeches had a hypnotic effect on the crowds. In fact, since he had no formal education and was born in Austria to a father who was of no notable standing, it has always amazed me that he became Chancellor of Germany. It should be noted that it was not just his ability to speak that accounts for his influence, however, but the fact that he was able to direct toward the Jewish population the anger felt by the German people over their loss in World War I. That is, he capitalized on an emotion that they already felt and showed them how they could right the wrongs that had been done to them.

Since there are large volumes written on communication, it is not my intention to go into great depth on the subject but to touch on those aspects of communication that I believe a project leader should know—especially those skills that are needed for effectiveness as a leader.

COMMUNICATION OF RELATIONSHIP

Every communication contains two components. There is the content or message conveyed, and there is a definition of the relationship that the communicator sees herself as having with the other person. For example, if I say to someone, "Hand me that piece of paper," I am conveying a relationship of familiarity and possibly of being of higher status than the other person.

On the other hand, if I say, "Would you hand me that paper?" I am conveying the same message, but now the relationship is defined as more equal status.

Equal-status relationships are called symmetrical, whereas unequal-status relationships are called complementary. The nature of symmetrical relationships is unstable, as each person will constantly be seeing evidence that the relationship is actually unequal at the moment. The best that one can expect is that they will be equal on the average! If the expectation is for the relationship to be of equal status at all times, there is no way this expectation can be met, and most likely the difference will eventually cause a rift.

Every communication contains two components

- *contents or message conveyed*
- *definition of the relationship*

Complementary relationships are stable unless one person wants to turn the relationship into a symmetrical one. This is sometimes called a power struggle, and we will address this issue later on.

Now suppose I communicate in such a way that the relationship definition that I offer the other person is unacceptable. For example, if I communicate with my boss as though we were equal-status, she may be offended. On the other hand, if I communicate with a peer or co-worker as though I see our relationship as unequal-status (complementary), he may also be offended and reply, "Who made you my boss?"

So we see that it is not so much what we say as the way we say it that counts, because the way we say it defines our relationship with the other person.

DEFINITION AS THE SOURCE OF CONFLICT

Unless both parties in a relationship accept the definition, there will be conflict. In a male-female relationship, for example, if one person wants to define the situation as romantic while the other person just wants to be friends, then you know that conflict will be the result.

Another example of this that can be humorous is having a total stranger approach you at a party and start pouring out his soul to you. His wife has just left him and taken the kids, the dog, and the checkbook, and the poor fellow is devastated. The only reason he has come to the party is to drink himself into a mindless state so he can escape the reality of his dreadful life at the moment.

Nevertheless, his outpouring of very personal information defines his relationship with you as close and personal, whereas in reality you are strangers. This mismatch between the definition he offers and the reality causes you to feel considerable discomfort, and to try to either redefine the relationship or to simply escape as quickly as possible.

For project managers, this relationship definition issue can be very important because you are often in a situation in which the people on your team are not "your" people. They have been assigned from various functional groups, either on a temporary basis or as a matrix project, in which case they still report to their functional managers.

In such situations, you must use influence to get things done, and you cannot successfully influence someone if you define your relationship with him in a way that he rejects. Generally, this means that you must request, rather than direct. You must persuade, rather than order. And sometimes you must beg!

INFORMATION AND MEANING

The next thing we must consider is that information and meaning are not the same thing. The statement "Two plus two is four," will mean something totally different to a two-year-old, a six-year-old, and an adult. The two-year old may find the statement totally incomprehensible. The six-year-old will understand what it means but will relate it strictly to newly learned math. The adult may wonder why you are telling her this or what hidden message you are trying to convey. Do you think she is stupid? Are you making a joke? What is going on?

One of the tenets of NLP (this is short for neuro-linguistic programming) is that the meaning of a communication is the response it gets. It makes no difference what you intend to convey, it is what the other person actually hears that determines how he or she will respond. If you tell a woman that two plus two is four and she hears that as an implication that she is stupid, then she is going to respond with indignation. The fact that you were simply "thinking out loud" to yourself upon finding that you added incorrectly in your checkbook does not matter. She is now angry at you, and you will have to explain what you were doing.

Consider another situation. You are trying to explain something to a group. One member is totally baffled. You think you communicated well because everyone else in the group seems to be with you.

That's fine, but you have one person who is not "getting it," and if you want to reach this person, you're going to have to communicate in a different way. Perhaps you must backtrack to something that preceded your explanation. You may need to lay some groundwork before the person can understand.

Whatever the case, the mode in which you communicated to the group as a whole is not working for this one individual, and you will have to vary your approach.

This leads to another NLP tenet: The responsibility for communication rests with the communicator, not the receiver! For many people, this is hard to swallow. We have learned to consider anyone who doesn't understand our clear communication as dense; that is, we blame them if they don't understand. Now we're told that we must take responsibility for that person's being able to understand. That seems just a bit too much!

As a project manager, however, you must ask yourself what your desired outcome is. Do you want to be self-righteous and continue to have a person in your team who doesn't understand, or do you want to get the message across so that he understands you? The choice is yours.

HOW TO COMMUNICATE EFFECTIVELY

If you want to communicate effectively, there are three rules you must follow:

 1. Communicate.
 2. Have the sensitivity to know if you got the desired result.
 3. Have the flexibility to change your approach until you do get the desired result.

Have you ever met someone who was abrasive or in some way disagreeable to deal with, and who seemed to have no clue that this was true? In other words, the person had no idea what effect his or her behavior was having on other people.

No doubt you have seen instructors or professors who seemed oblivious to the fact that most of their students were lost. This is why rule two above is so important.

Rule three, however, is the one that also seems to be overlooked by such people. If you say to them, "I'm sorry, but I don't understand what you just said," there is a good chance that the brilliant instructor will just offer the same explanation in the very same words that he or she used the first time! It makes you want to scream, "If those words had worked, I would have understood the first time. For goodness sake, use different words!"

One really prevalent example of this is when adults try to communicate with children. When the child doesn't understand, the adult tells the child to "Act more grown up." This is ridiculous. If the child were more grown up, he or she would have understood in the first place. So another rule for dealing with people is that you must deal with them where they are, not where you want them to be.

In the case of children, this means that you must communicate on the child's level, not on an adult level.

HOW PEOPLE PROCESS INFORMATION

We all gather and process information through our five physical senses: vision, hearing, taste, touch, and smell. Ideally, each of us should be able to process information in all five modes

Processing information

We all gather and process information through our five physical senses:

- *vision*
- *hearing*
- *taste*
- *touch*
- *smell*

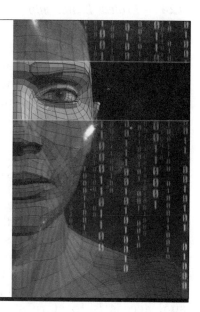

equally well, but this is not the case. Some people prefer to think in pictures. Others use sound (auditory) as the dominant mode. And still other individuals prefer the feeling mode (often called kinesthetic).

As an example, think of "coffee." What comes to mind?

Did you see a cup of coffee?

Did you hear the sound of coffee brewing, either percolating or dripping through the filter?

Did you have a sensation of smelling that strong coffee aroma that we associate with mornings?

Or did you have a feeling? Or think of the taste of freshly brewed coffee?

No matter how you did it, as a single mode or a combination of them, you were thinking in one or more sensory modes.

To summarize, the different ways of thinking are:

Visual. You think in pictures. You represent ideas, memory, and imagination as mental images.

Auditory. You think in sounds. You may talk to yourself, hear the sounds of musical instruments or songs, or other noises.

Feeling. You represent thoughts as feelings that might be internal emotion or the thought of a physical touch. People with a strong preference for feelings must experience something to understand it.

EYE-ACCESSING CUES TO THINKING

It turns out that you can tell which mode a person is using at a given moment by watching the movement of his or her eyes. When the eyes go upward, the person is thinking in pictures. If the direction is to the person's right (your left when facing him), the person is constructing images in his head. If his eyes move to his left (your right), he is remembering an image he has seen before. Another visual access is to stare straight ahead with the eyes slightly defocused. This can be either remembered or created images.

When the eyes move horizontally left or right, this is auditory. When the eyes move to the person's left (your right), she is remembering a sound, perhaps someone's voice. If the eyes go to her right, she is thinking about how to say something. Finally, if her eyes go down to her left, she is having an internal dialog.

Finally, if a person's eyes move down to his right, he is accessing his feelings about something. This is called the kinesthetic access. The various positions taken by the eyes are shown in Figure 9.1.

LANGUAGE AND THINKING MODE

The language we use also gives a cue to the mode in which we are thinking. A person who is thinking in pictures will use expressions such as:

- ❏ "I see what you mean."
- ❏ "It doesn't look right to me."
- ❏ "I don't like the looks of it."

For auditory thinking, we have:

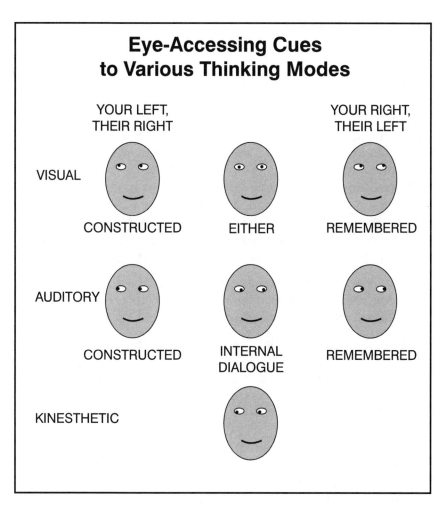

Figure 9.1
Eye-accessing cues.

- ❏ "It sounds like a good deal to me."
- ❏ "It rings true."
- ❏ "It's music to my ears!"

And for kinesthetic, you might hear:

- ❏ "I feel really bad about what happened."
- ❏ "I can't get a handle on it."
- ❏ "I feel positively nauseated when I think about it."

WHY DOES IT MATTER?

No doubt you are wondering why any of this matters. It's simple. You can't have effective communication with a person, nor can you influence or persuade them, unless you first have rapport with them.

Notice the definition says that each person has a sense that the other person understands and shares his concerns. This is vitally important. Any time you feel that another person does not care about what concerns you, then you have no basis for a friendly, cooperative relationship. In fact, one of the definitions of conflict is that:

> Conflict occurs when one person or party frustrates the concerns of another person or party. Concerns include values, objectives, or other interests held by a person.

Since almost all negotiations suggest that there is a conflict between the parties involved, it is important that a manager knows how to establish rapport with the person he is negotiating with if he wants to achieve a successful outcome. Further, it is necessary to have rapport with others in order to communicate effectively with them.

Now remember that perceived differences between people automatically create the impression that "you don't understand me because we're different."

Also remember how we started this chapter discussing the content and relationship aspects of communication, and we said that every communication conveys a definition of relationship. So if there is no rapport between two people, each will see the relationship as unfriendly, uncooperative, and unpalatable.

For this reason, it is extremely important to develop rapport with the other person before trying to influence her in any way. One way to do this is to communicate with her in the thinking mode that she most prefers. If she is visually oriented, then you need to talk the language of images, draw pictures for her, or show her diagrams that help her understand your points.

For someone who is predominantly kinesthetic, you need to talk about feelings, help the person experience what you are trying to convey, or actually "walk him through it." For example, if you were trying to convince him to buy a car, you would want to take him out for a test drive so he could experience the feeling of the car firsthand.

Similarly, for a person who is predominantly auditory, you need to communicate in an auditory mode yourself.

The point is that by listening to how people talk, and by adding to that observation of their eye movements, you can determine the preferred mode(s) in which they process information and match your own communication to their preferred mode.

MATCHING AND PACING

Have you ever noticed what happens when two people naturally have established rapport with each other, perhaps at a party or some other social event? They become very comfortable and relaxed. There will be a lot of head nodding to acknowledge the other person. Furthermore, they will match each other's body posture.

For example, if they are standing facing each other, and one person stands with her body tilted slightly to the side, the other person will either tilt his body in the same direction or possibly tilt his body in a mirror image. This is an unconscious process, but by adopting it consciously, you will find that you can build rapport very quickly with another person.

After you have "matched" the other person's body and language, you can lead the person in the direction you want to take him. This is called "matching" and "pacing." It is a necessary ingredient of influence.

In the situation described above, there is not a direct one-for-one correspondence between their body postures, and yet there is a sense of comfort between them.

This sort of thing occurs naturally all the time. The thing for us to do as managers is gain conscious control over the process so we can use it in leading people.

SYMBOLIC COMMUNICATION

Before we go further, we should note an aspect of communication that is often overlooked. Verbal communication is conveyed by words themselves. Nonverbal communication is conveyed by body movements, posture, and the inflections or tone of voice one uses. We sometimes say that the verbal component is digital in nature and the nonverbal is analog.

There is another mode of communication that we need to account for, and it is called symbolic. The Smothers Brothers once did a little song, to the tune of "The Streets of Laredo," that went:

> *Tommy: I see by your outfit that you are a cowboy.*
>
> *Dick: I see by your outfit that you're a cowboy too.*
>
> *Both: We see by our outfits that we are both cowboys. If you get an outfit, you can be a cowboy too.*

This little ditty illustrates in a very abbreviated way a principle we are all aware of, but that we sometimes forget: The way you choose to dress, comb your hair, and adorn your body signals to other people who you are. Every group has its own uniform. Skinheads look one way. Business executives look another. Programmers have their particular dress code. Catholic clergy wear a special collar. And so on. If each group had no such uniform, their members could not recognize each other. This symbolic communication even extends to possessions. BMW drivers often flash their headlights at other BMW drivers as a way of saying, "Hey, you're part of the in-group."

One of the problems with symbolic communication is that it can make rapport extremely difficult to establish because two people who are dressed very differently see each other as so different that they believe the other person cannot possibly relate to or understand them. Remember, rapport is based on a mutual feeling of similarity, and perceived differences destroy or prevent rapport from ever developing.

So if you choose to look different than the people you want to relate to, be aware that those differences will be a barrier to the very relationship that you want to establish.

It is increasingly important that project managers understand differences in how people communicate in different cultures.

CROSS-CULTURAL DIFFERENCES

As projects become more global in nature, it becomes increasingly important that project managers understand differences in how people communicate in different cultures. Even within the United States there are differences that lead to misunderstandings and conflict. People from the northeast tend to be more direct-spoken than southerners, and when they interact, the southern person is sometimes offended by that direct-spoken manner. Conversely, the person from the north is annoyed that the southerner "beats around the bush." He wonders why this slow-talking person doesn't get to the point and say what he means.

Internationally, the differences become even more difficult. We Americans like to deal with each other on a first-name basis, so we go to European countries like Germany and call senior managers by their first names. The German manager may find this very offensive, unless he has had a lot of dealings with Americans and has learned to tolerate their rude behavior.

Note that term: Anyone who violates your cultural norms is considered to be behaving rudely!

As an example, an American businessman closed a very large deal with a British company. The British manager said, "Well, now, why don't we celebrate by having a glass of sherry."

The American replied that he would like to, but he really needed to get back to his hotel and prepare for his trip back to the United States the following day. When he got back to his hotel, there was a message from the British manager:

> *The deal is off. If you don't have time to have a glass of sherry with me, it means that all you care about is my money, and I don't do business that way!*

This is by no means an isolated incident. Many business relationships have been destroyed by violations of cultural expectations. So if you want to avoid such problems, you should read as much as you can on the differences that exist in whatever country you are dealing with. One excellent reference is Morrison, Conaway and Borden, 1994.

READING NONVERBAL BEHAVIOR

We have all been told that a person sitting with arms crossed may be "closed off" to whatever is taking place around her. You may have a hard time reaching her. The problem is, arms folded across the chest doesn't always mean a person is closed off. It may simply mean she is comfortable, or even chilly!

As an example of a cross-cultural problem with body language, there are parts of India in which a person will shake his head from side-to-side in a way that looks to an American like he is saying "no." However, what he is really signaling is more like "I'm with you."

So here is the message: There is only one way to know for sure what someone's body language is saying, and that is to check it out! If, for example, you thought that the person with arms crossed was closed off, you can simply ask, "Are you with me?" Or you may say, "I'm concerned that you're not with me. Tell me what you're thinking right now."

If you find that she is indeed closed off, then you can deal with her appropriately. On the other hand, if she was just being comfortable, there is nothing you need to do—she is already with you.

10

Interpersonal Influence

Leadership is essentially an influence process, so the more you know about how to persuade people to do something, the more likely you will be to get the results you are after. Furthermore, since good communication skills are required to be able to influence effectively, if you have not read the previous chapter, I suggest that this is the time to go back and read it before continuing with this chapter.

All communication can be thought of as a way of influencing others. In some cases, you are trying to get them to simply understand you. Or you may want something from them. Or you want them to do something that needs to be done. You may also be trying to make an impression. Whatever the motive, communication influences, and, since you can't *not* communicate, you also can't not influence! That's right, you can't avoid communicating. Even silence communicates.

Consider, for example, being seated beside someone on a plane who never speaks to you. Is he communicating? You bet! What is he communicating about his relationship with you?

Simple: He doesn't want to have one!

THE SIX CATEGORIES OF INFLUENCE METHODS

Influence is the process of getting another person to change his or her attitudes, beliefs, values, or behavior. There are many ways to do this, but they usually fall into one of six categories, each of which is governed by a basic psychological principle that directs our behavior. These principles are consistency, reciprocation, social proof, conformity, liking, and scarcity.

Commitment and Consistency

The principle involved here is that, once a person makes a decision, he or she will behave consistently with that commitment. To illustrate, suppose you are buying a new car; you have taken a test drive in several cars, and you have made your choice. The salesperson has told you the price for the car. You go inside to do the paperwork, and when the salesperson hands you the papers, the price on the invoice is a few hundred dollars higher than you were quoted out on the lot. What do you do? You probably protest, but the salesperson explains that the quote was just a ballpark and did not include prep charges. There is a good chance that most people will grit their teeth and sign the papers. Why, they had already committed to buying the car. Perhaps also, they weigh the cost of starting over versus absorbing the few hundred dollars, which will be spread over the total payment span.

For leaders, then, this means that if you can get a person to make a commitment, you can expect him or her to follow through. This is one reason why it is better to have people actually "sign up" for a project rather than being "drafted." When they make a

All relationships are exchange relationships.

commitment by joining, they are much more likely to perform well, support the project, and speak highly of the experience.

There is also a principle in psychology called cognitive dissonance, which has to do with the uncertainty one faces when making choices. Once you have bought that new car, you will actually read more ads for that particular model than you did before you bought it. What you are doing is trying to convince yourself that you did the right thing, thus reducing the anxiety you felt about making a choice that was not 100 percent certain to be the right one.

Equity, Reciprocity, and Influence

Consider two people in a relationship: Call them A and B. Equity theory asserts that they will try to keep their outcomes proportional to their inputs. That is, each person expects to derive benefits from the relationship in proportion to what she puts into it. She also expects the ratio of output to input to be about equal. If the ratios are not about equal, then the person receiving the smallest number of outcomes is likely to view the situation as unfair. She is giving more to the relationship and getting proportionately less for it than the other person. If this disparity is not corrected, you could expect her to break off the relationship.

Another way to say this is that all relationships are exchange relationships, and if the exchanges between the individuals do not meet expectations, then the relationship may decay. A simple example of this is when one person finds that he has invited the other person to attend an event with him 10 times but the other person has never invited him to attend an event. "What does this mean?" the person asks himself. Perhaps it means that the other person doesn't care as much about him as he does about the other person. That being the conclusion, the relationship soon ends.

Reciprocity

One aspect of this is reciprocity. You do a favor for someone. Later on, you need a favor from her. If she grants the favor, you are satisfied with the relationship. Otherwise, you cry "foul"—unless the person has very extenuating circumstances that legitimately prevent her reciprocating. She has not lived up to her end of the "bargain."

Reciprocation is one of the most effective means of influence because the sense of obligation is generally very strong. Charitable organizations try to use this sense of obligation by sending out address labels for which they solicit donations. One organization has found that a simple solicitation for contributions usually nets them about an 18 percent response rate. If they include the "gift" address labels, that rate nearly doubles, to 35 percent.

Social Norms and Social Proof

Norms are expected modes of behavior and belief established by a group. They facilitate interaction by specifying what is expected and acceptable behavior in a particular situation. Norms make life easier for us. They allow us to predict with some accuracy how others will behave, and they keep us from having to always decide how to act ourselves.

As an example of a norm, each culture has its own expectation for how far apart people stand when talking. In some societies, that distance is so close that the two people can literally smell each other's breath. In American society, that proximity is too close, and we feel uncomfortable when someone moves in so close to us, unless it is a person with whom we have a romantic or family tie.

Our instinct is to move back, to restore the "proper" distance from the other person. However, this breaks rapport with him, so he moves back in. This constant retreat-advance-retreat-advance interaction leaves both parties feeling uncomfortable. His norms have been violated (as have yours), and he may well tell members of his own group how rude the person from the other group was. Norms not only establish expectations for behavior but for dress codes as well. A newly hired manager asked the president of the company about the company's dress code. The president informed him that there was no dress code.

"Of course there is," said the new manager. "Everyone wears white shirts and ties." There may not have been an official dress code, but there certainly was an unofficial one that had been developed unconsciously. People simply observe others (this is called social comparison) to find out what they believe are the rules they are supposed to follow, and they unconsciously establish norms.

Social proof has to do with our belief that if everyone else is doing it, it must be right. So if everyone else has suddenly started having the hair on one side of their head dyed green, you may eventually comply with the majority behavior and have your own hair dyed.

Conformity

Groups exert enormous pressure on their members to conform to those group norms. Failure of a person to abide by group expectations may well result in her being expelled from the group. A member of a street gang may be expelled for being "too good," for example, or for performing too well in school. That person is conforming to the rules of the "out group," not the gang itself.

One of the most famous experiments to demonstrate the power of group pressure to conform was conducted by Solomon Asch. He brought together from seven to nine individuals to take part in "an experiment in visual discrimination." They were told to match the length of a standard line with one of three comparison lines drawn on a card and to announce their judgments in the order in which they were seated.

All but one person in the group were actually confederates of the experimenter. The one naive subject was always seated next-to-last in the lineup. The other members had been instructed to respond incorrectly on certain trials. At those times, the confederates would deliberately choose the wrong line for the match. That is, it was clearly not the same length as the standard line, but they would all say that it was. An example of one of Asch's cards is shown in Figure 10.1.

So, using this figure as an example, the confederates would all say that the line nearest in length to the standard was line 1, which is clearly not true. However, by the time the actual subject had heard six people claim that line one was correct, many would say the same thing.

Asch found that subjects resisted group influence on about two-thirds of the (incorrect) trials and yielded on the remaining third. Interestingly, about five percent of subjects agreed with the group on every trial, about one-fourth "stuck to their guns" and made no errors at all, and another third agreed with the group on half or more of the trials.

In debriefing subjects, Asch found that some of them actually doubted their vision after hearing six other people give an incorrect response. After all, they thought, it was an experiment in perception, so maybe there was something about themselves that made them see the lines differently than the majority.

Asch also found that only three confederates were necessary to gain conformity. The implications of this are profound. If you hear only three people say something that isn't true, you are inclined to believe them. The implication for juries is especially compelling.

External and Internal Compliance

It is important to understand that people may say that two lines are the same without actually accepting their statement as true. In doing so, they are concerned with how the group sees them, but internally, they know the group is wrong.

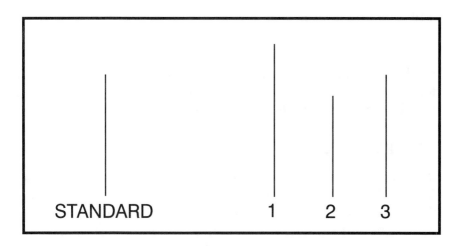

Figure 10.1
Asch's cards.

What this means for project managers is that you must be careful not to let your team put pressure on a person with a "weird idea" to give it up. It may well be that the weird idea is actually correct, and you will lose both it and the person's commitment to the group if you let them overrule him without engaging in open discussion about the issue.

Liking

It isn't surprising that we most prefer to say yes to the requests we get from people we know and like. This is the secret of Tupperware sales. The company has their salespeople invite their friends to a Tupperware party. It is much harder to say no to your friend than to a salesperson who is a stranger.

Scarcity

Ever notice how many of these in-your-face TV ads end by saying, "Place your order now because quantities are limited." Sure, they are limited to several warehouses full of product. But if they have convinced you that not everyone will get in on this special deal—so that if you do, you are a member of a select few—then you feel pressure not to be left out. I have even heard this tactic used to get a person to take a promotion he really didn't want by telling him that there might not be too many more opportunities like this one, so he shouldn't pass it up.

The Word "Because"

Researchers have found that you greatly increase the likelihood that another person will grant a request if you say, "Could you do this for me *because* . . ." followed by an explanation. In other words, if you provide a justification for your request—and especially if that justification is reasonable—you increase the probability of compliance.

The really surprising thing is that just saying *because* without giving a reason also increases compliance above that which you get by just making a request. It is not clear why this should be true, but it is (Cialdini, 1993).

The message here is that if you want people to comply with your directives or requests as a manager, be sure to give them a reason.

POWER AND INFLUENCE

If you are able to get others to do things you think should be done, there is a sense in which you have power over them. The question is, what do we mean by *power,* and how does it work?

French and Raven (1959) outlined five bases of power that allow leaders to influence others. In 1976, Raven and Rubin identified a sixth kind of power, information, which has become increasingly important in recent years. (See Table 10.1.)

Reward Power

This is a form of power that most project managers believe they do not have because they tend to think of it as money. True, you generally can't give people raises or other pay incentives as a project manager, but you have the most valuable of all assets to give

Power and Its Bases	
Reward	Derives from being in a position to administer rewards that a follower desires.
Coercive	The ability of a leader to punish followers for not complying with a directive.
Legitimate	Power granted to a person based on his or her position in the organization.
Referent	The power leaders gain when people identify with them.
Expert	The leader has important knowledge or expertise about an activity being performed.
Information	This is similar to expert power, but even if the person does not know how to perform an activity, his information may still give him power over others.

Table 10.1

followers—appreciation, as I have said previously. The nice thing about such intangible rewards is that the people who receive them are virtually insatiable, so the rewards seldom lose their effectiveness, unless the follower thinks you are insincere, and then your compliments will backfire.

Coercive Power

Even if you had this power, which most managers do not have, you would find that it is an extremely poor way to get things done because once you have used it a single time, you will find that from then on, it is the *only* way you will get people to do anything. Most importantly, in today's world, there are very few employees who allow managers to coerce them into doing anything.

I once had a prison warden tell me that the prison officials all understood that the inmates stayed there by choice. They may not have come there by choice, but once there, they remained. I didn't understand, so he said, "There are a lot more of them than there are of us. If they ever decide they aren't staying, we will have a very difficult time holding them." If this is true of prison inmates, think how much more true it is of employees.

In today's world, there are very few employees who allow managers to coerce them to do anything.

Legitimate Power

In organizations that have weak project management structures, the project leader has very little legitimate power. This is why many people advocate that project managers be elevated to a position equivalent to that of the functional managers from whom they receive their team members. In addition, Graham and Englund (1997) have suggested that the organization adopt the position that functional groups exist only to serve the needs of projects, since as much as 80 percent of all work is done in projects. By doing this, the project manager is given greater legitimate power.

Referent Power

In Chapter 3 I said that one of the Kouzes and Posner practices was for leaders to lead by example—to be role models for others to follow. Without doing this, you have no referent power. It is also a fragile power because if a leader does something that is immoral, unethical, or rude, he or she may lose the respect of followers, and in so doing lose referent power.

Expert Power

In multidisciplinary projects, there is some limit to this form of power because a leader is unlikely to have extensive knowledge in all areas of the project. However, it doesn't have to be technical expertise—if the leader is perceived as an expert in political maneuvering or in managing projects, this may be enough. It depends in part on the group. In any case, it is only accorded to a person if the group values it. For example, if I am an expert in psychology but my team does not value this expertise, then I get no credit for having it.

Information Power

This form of power is becoming more important in this age of information. In fact, Dr. Peter Drucker has written that the economics of scarcity no longer apply as much in an information economy. This is because the more people have certain information, the more valuable it becomes.

I have seen this with project management. When I started teaching *Leadership Skills for Project Managers* in 1980, there were very few seminars being offered on basic project management. Not too many people had yet realized the value of the discipline, so the information was not something you could readily sell.

That has all changed. Last year, three companies in the United States did a combined 140 million dollars in project management training, and they are just the three I have some data for. All of a sudden, information about how to manage projects has monetary value because a lot of people have it, which causes even more people to want it.

LEADERSHIP PRINCIPLES

Like Kouzes and Posner, Robert Rosen (1996) has conducted extensive research on leadership, and has identified eight principles that leaders must practice if they are to get people to follow them.

The energy of the organization is the participation and effort of the people. And leaders pay close attention to people's talent.

These are vision, trust, participation, learning, diversity, creativity, integrity, and community.

- ❏ **Vision.** Leaders see the whole picture and articulate that broad perspective to others. By doing so, leaders create a common purpose that mobilizes people and coordinates their efforts into a single, coherent, agile enterprise.

- ❏ **Trust.** Without trust, vision becomes an empty slogan. Trust binds people together, creating a strong, resilient organization. To build trust, leaders are predictable, and they share information and power. Their goal is a culture of candor.

- ❏ **Participation.** The energy of an organization is the participation and effort of its people. The leader's challenge is to unleash and focus this energy, inspiring people at every level of the enterprise to pitch in with their minds and hearts.

- ❏ **Learning.** Leaders need a deep understanding of themselves. They must know their strengths and shortcomings, which requires a lifelong process of discovery, and they must be able to adapt to new circumstances. So too with their organization. It must promote constant innovation, and the leaders must encourage their people to refresh their skills and renew their spirits.

❑ **Diversity.** Successful leaders know the power of diversity and the poison of prejudice. They understand their own biases, and they actively cultivate an appreciation of the positive aspects of people's differences. In their organizations, they insist on a culture of mutual respect.

❑ **Creativity.** In a world where smart solutions outpace excessive work, creativity is crucial. Leaders pay close attention to people's talents, leaning on their strengths and managing around their weaknesses. They encourage independent, challenging thinking, and they invest in technologies that facilitate the efforts of their people.

❑ **Integrity.** A leader must stand for something. As a public citizen and a private person, she knows what is important in life and acts by deep-seated principles. Every wise leader has a moral compass, a sense of right and wrong. Good leaders understand that good ethics is good business.

❑ **Community.** Community is mutual commitment, and it inspires the highest performance. It's human nature to go the extra mile for one's neighbors and fellow citizens, and a mature leader stresses the organization's responsibility to the surrounding society. A leader also acts as a steward of the natural environment (Rosen, 1996, pp. 21–22).

11

Mulally's Principles for Managing

*I*n 2000, I *watched* the PBS video, *21st Century Jet,* which documented development of the 777 airplane by Boeing. I was so impressed with the management of that huge program that I contacted Alan Mulally, who had initially been chief engineer of the job and was now president of Boeing Commercial Airplanes, and asked if I could interview him. He consented, and during that meeting, he shared with me 12 principles that guide him in managing projects, teams, and the corporation itself. I later wrote a book about these principles, entitled *Working Together*. For this book, I would like to simply share with you Mulally's principles, with a brief explanation of each, because I think they are essential guidelines for any project leader to follow.

Working Together

The overall "umbrella" for Mulally's principles is the philosophy of working together. When the 777 program began, the practice at Boeing had been similar to that of most product development organizations: Marketing developed specifications and threw them over the wall to engineering, who then developed the product and threw drawings over the wall to manufacturing, who then threw the product over the wall to the customer—who, needless to say, was totally surprised by what was delivered. But Don Peterson, president of Ford Motor Company, was a member of Boeing's board of directors, and he suggested that Mulally talk with Lew Viraldi about how he was managing the new Ford project to develop the Taurus automobile.

This project was a new approach for Ford. Rather than practicing throw-it-over-the-wall, they were actually involving all stakeholders in the program from concept through completion. They had, for example, assembly workers on the team, as well as ordinary people who drive cars, as well as engineers and suppliers. In their discussions, Viraldi convinced Mulally that this approach should be followed in developing the 777.

Most notably, the customer was a major part of the design team. In this case, that customer was a representative from United Airlines, who had agreed to purchase a certain number of airplanes if they met their requirements. Naturally, their representative was there to ensure that the plan would meet United's needs when it was finished.

To make a long story short, the approach proved so successful that the phrase "Working Together" was screened on the nose of the first 777 to come off the assembly line, and it is displayed prominently on the wall outside Mulally's office. Although it seems obvious that no complex product can be designed by a single individual, getting people to actually practice the working together principles is more difficult than might be imagined.

Compelling Vision

Since leadership is the art of getting people to want to do something you believe should be done, it follows that you can only lead them to a destination to which they want to go.

*Ignoring the power of **vision** is failing to tap into one of the most powerful drivers of all.*

People are driven to achieve grand visions. We see this in countless examples—from Stonehenge to the pyramids of Egypt and Central America, to the World Trade Center, and to the giant corporations that are the modern counterpart of these great buildings. You see

Without vision, the people perish.

it also in the scientists who devote their lives to developing drugs to save humanity from devastating diseases—Jonas Salk with polio, for example. You witness it in race car drivers who want to go faster and faster, and in musicians who want to become perfect in the performance of their music.

A leader who ignores the power of vision is failing to tap into one of the most powerful drivers of all. Churchill created a vision for the people of a country that would survive the German blitz and rise victorious from the ashes like the giant Phoenix of mythology. And John F. Kennedy and Martin Luther King, Jr., in more recent times have used vision as a way of inspiring followers. Martin Luther King's famous "I Have a Dream" speech is a perfect example of the power of vision to energize people to pursue a goal.

Everyone Is Included

Leaders usually have an inner circle of friends and advisors, but they also try to make time to talk with anyone who wants an audience. When they make speeches, they constantly scan the audience, making everyone feel included. They talk the language of "we," as I have written previously. They empower people, rather than practicing disempowering methods.

Exclusionary tactics, in which only the "chosen" have access to the leader, make people feel left out, disempowered, and of limited worth, and ultimately cause them to seek out a leader who will show them respect. And this is sometimes the style of corporate leaders, whether consciously or by reason of their tremendously busy schedules, which limit the time they can give to their employees. I have observed that those CEOs who seem to somehow find time for anyone who wants an audience are loved and respected, and their followers are willing to do almost anything for them.

This does not mean that every employee is included in absolutely everything in a direct way, but I believe it does mean that to the degree possible, they are all made to feel that they contribute to the greater good of the company, that they are all valued for those contributions, and that the corporate hierarchy does not grant higher-level managers any greater worth than it grants those at lower levels.

Clear Performance Goals

To achieve a vision, various goals must be established and achieved as well. People need to know what they are to do, how their performance will be measured, and how they will be rewarded. I have said previously that most of us work to please our supervisors, and people want to know what the leader's goals are, so that they can pursue them and gain that appreciation. When leaders send mixed signals about the direction in which they are heading or, worse yet, send no signals at all, people become confused, aimless, and uninspired. There is not much point in following a person who seems to be going nowhere!

One Plan

Every organization tries to achieve its overall vision, and this can only be done if there is a unified master plan that coordinates the work of all groups. When every department is pursuing its own objectives, without regard for whether they align with the master goal, you have an organization that is fragmented and headed for disintegration.

It is the leader's job to facilitate development of this master plan. In large part, it is a matter of ensuring that the compelling vision is a shared vision—one that everyone understands and embraces. Further, each department should understand their role in achieving that vision, so that they can produce a plan that meshes with the master.

The Data Sets Us Free

I saw a TV program once that reported a study of conversations among people in which they found that perhaps 60 to 80 percent of the conversation was gossip. We seem to love to gossip, to talk about other people and what they are doing, especially if their behavior has an unusual aspect to it. In organizations, this conversation is called "water cooler talk," and conveys the same idea. What is such-and-such an employee or manager doing? Is the company on safe ground, or are we headed for trouble?

People want to be "in the know" about things. The problem is that if they don't have actual facts available to them they rely on rumors for their knowledge. Most importantly, they act on what they believe to be the facts.

For that reason, people must be kept informed about what is really true, meaning that they must be given actual data, whether it be financial, market, or other performance statistics. I remember that in the early days of the quality movement, companies found that their employees did not believe they had quality problems. They thought that managers were just trying to scare them into doing more work for the same pay. So companies were forced to start sharing "hard" data with their people to convince them that they did have problems. This broke the ice and they were able to move forward. Proper responses to problems can only be made if data is available that reveals the actual condition of the situation, so that people are not reacting to guesswork and fear.

You Can't Manage a Secret

There are managers who react to bad news by "shooting the messenger." When people find out that this is the person's style, they hide problems as best they can, revealing them only when it is impossible to keep them secret any longer. Good leaders welcome bad news—not because they are happy about the bad news, but because they know that the only way to solve a problem is to first know that it exists. Dr. Deming said that employees should be rewarded for revealing problems for that very reason.

An effective leader responds to such news by asking what can be done about it. He or she is focused on solving the problem, not bewailing that it exists, not berating employees for their stupidity or their causing it, or promising to find out who is responsible and punishing him.

Whining Is Okay—Occasionally

We all have times when we feel so much pain or grief that we need a "shoulder to cry on." Good leaders know this and allow us to vent occasionally. I believe that a person who cannot empathize with others—especially their pain—will be ineffective as a leader. For that reason, a leader must be willing to let people vent without putting them down with remarks like, "That's just an excuse."

We hold to the myth that "real men" don't feel pain and grief, but if you observe those men whom most of us consider to be good leaders, you see expressions of pain and sorrow. Giuliani felt great pain in the aftermath of the terrorist attack, and he did not hesitate to show it. Churchill said he had only "blood, sweat, toil and tears" to offer his people.

Still, we must move on. Once we have vented our emotion, we must solve the problem, and a good leader offers encouragement, hope, and help in moving forward. This is what people want from a leader—help in overcoming great pain. To withhold such assistance and moral support is to lose your sway with followers very quickly.

Propose a Plan, Find a Way

This principle goes hand-in-hand with the previous one. It may be okay to whine, but you are expected to propose a way out. Leaders may lend their moral support and help you get the resources you need to solve the problem, but they expect you to do your part in solving it. Good leaders actually encourage others to be leaders of their own efforts, whether these be projects or departments. In making their followers more competent, they also make them independent of the "herd" mentality. As Kouzes and Posner found in their research, good leaders lead by example, showing their followers how to emulate their behavior in order to become self-sufficient.

Listen to Each Other and Help Each Other

One of the illnesses of organizations is the silo mentality. Groups decide that they exist to support their own objectives, separate from those of the rest of the company. They then do not help others. They compete rather than cooperate. When this happens, the organization is headed for disaster.

Mulally tries very hard to promote the value of mutual respect. We show respect for others when we listen to them, even when we disagree. As Covey wrote in his book *Seven Habits of Highly Effective People* (1989), "seek first to understand, then to be understood." This seems to be an increasingly important principle in our society today because there appears to be an erosion of respect for others. Perhaps it is because we are so busy, so frazzled, or so focused on achieving success that we are preoccupied with our own concerns, but we see many acts of indifference and disrespect.

One of these—at a simple level perhaps—is when people have side conversations in meetings, not listening to the person who is speaking. This is behavior that Mulally does not allow. If you must have a conversation, get up and leave the room. Don't do it while someone else is speaking.

Finally, cooperation is the cornerstone of a successful endeavor. No individual can achieve lofty goals alone. It requires the collective efforts of many people. So helping each other is not just a nice thing to do—it is mandatory!

Emotional Resilience

Everyone has setbacks. As the whining principle says, it is okay to whine a little, but you must recover and move on. For leaders, this is especially important. As Mulally told me in a personal conversation, if the leader reacts to bad news by falling down on the floor and kicking and screaming, team members really get worried. The world must be coming to an end.

This places a burden on leaders to keep their chins up in the worst of circumstances, as Giuliani and Churchill did in their times of crisis. It is okay to admit the pain you feel—that says you are human—but your response to pain is what counts, and that response must be positive.

I recently heard Mary McBride speak. She wrote jokes for Phyllis Diller for many years, and she said that she had been diagnosed with incurable cancer over 10 years earlier. Her response? "I'm going to live." And perhaps most importantly, she responded with humor. "The good thing about an incurable disease," she said, "is that you don't have to turn the cushions on your sofa. And you don't have to listen to the safety announcement on an airplane." Then, with a beautiful smile, she said, "And you don't care if you catch a cold."

Finally, she said that on her 75th birthday, a friend came to visit and she told her, "I never thought I would make it to 75." Her friend agreed and said, "I waited until the last minute to buy you a birthday card."

Have Fun—Enjoy the Journey and Each Other

Mulally's last principle is one that I believe is so important in today's hurry-up world. We become so intensely focused on our work and so serious about it that, unlike Mary McBride, we can't

Have fun

___

Enjoy the journey and each other. This is very important in today's hurry-up world.

see the humor in our situations, nor do we appreciate others who are on the path with us.

Work should be fun. It may be burdensome at times, but overall it should be fun. If it isn't, you should ask yourself if you are in the right place. We all know that long-term stress has serious health and mental effects on people. The saying that "laughter is the best medicine" is absolutely true. Like Mary McBride, the writer Norman Cousins contributed greatly to his own recovery from a serious illness with laughter (Cousins, 1989). So I urge you to practice this principle, and if you are a leader, you should promote a climate for your followers to have fun and enjoy their teammates. One of the Kouzes and Posner principles, you may remember, is celebrate accomplishments. Have fun. Enjoy the journey and each other.

12

Emotional Intelligence

*M*ost *of us are* familiar with the IQ, or intelligence quotient. People who have high IQs usually do well in school—at least if they apply themselves. Certainly their high IQ gives them the ability to do well in school.

For leaders, IQ would help them master the technology and tools they need to handle various aspects of the job. However, Daniel Goleman and his associates have found that a far greater determinant of leadership success is *emotional intelligence:* how leaders handle themselves and their relationships (Goleman, et al, 2002). These findings do not refer to "soft" criteria only, such as how people feel in their jobs. They include financial results as well. For example, they found in a study of a large accounting firm that there was a direct link between profits and the emotional intelligence (EI) of partners.

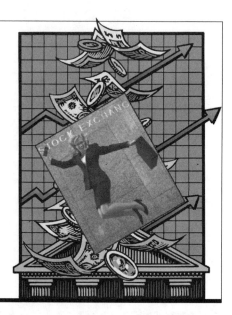

EI

In a study of a large accounting firm, there was a direct link between profits and the emotional intelligence of partners.

If the partner had significant strengths in the self-management competencies, he or she added 78 percent more incremental profit than did a partner without those strengths. Likewise, the added profits for partners with strengths in social skills were 110 percent greater, and those with strengths in the self-management competencies added a whopping 390 percent incremental profit—in this case, $1,465,000 more per year.

By contrast, significant strengths in analytic reasoning abilities added just 50 percent more profit. Thus, purely cognitive abilities help—but the EI competencies help far more (Goleman, et al, 2002, p. 251).

The soft criteria do count, but even when they appear to be "soft," there is usually a bottom-line impact when people are not happy with their leaders. For example, Goleman discusses the effect that the SOB boss has on people, and cites research that found that such bosses drive away talent. Study after study has found that people leave jobs primarily because of dissatisfaction with their boss. The Gallup Organization analyzed data obtained in interviews with over two million employees at 700 American companies and found that what determines how long employees stay in a job—and how productive they are—is the quality of their relationship with their immediate boss (Goleman, et al, 2002, p. 83).

When you consider that the cost to replace a factory worker is several thousand dollars and the cost for a professional can easily be several hundred thousand dollars, then the cost of such turnover has a direct effect on the bottom line. Yet many companies do not include this measure in the assessment of their managers—if they did, it would give them clear signs of which managers must reform or go.

EMOTIONS—IN THE WORKPLACE?

When I was a young engineer, I heard a number of managers admonish their employees to "leave your emotions at home," when they came to work. Yet they wanted these same employees to be motivated to do good work. Somehow they never realized that *emotion* and *motivate* both have the same root, which essentially means "to move." Being motivated is an emotional state. Rocks aren't motivated. People are.

Take away emotion and what are you left with? Either a rock or a zombie of an individual. In fact, consider the function of a compelling vision: it is to arouse passion in people. As the proverb says, "without vision the people perish." To quote Goleman, et al,

> *Great leaders move us. They ignite our passion and inspire the best in us. When we try to explain why they are so effective, we speak of strategy, vision, or powerful ideas. But the reality is much more primal: Great leadership works on the emotions (Goleman, et al, 2002, p. 3).*

They go on to say that, no matter what the leader tries to do, the leader's success depends on *how* she or he does it. Even if a leader gets everything else right, if she or he fails to drive emotions in the right direction, nothing will be done as well as it could be.

In every instance that I can remember in which someone has told me about working at a great company or on a challenging project, the core has always been the same: There was great excitement generated. People were energized by their work, they were driven to achieve grand results, and they expended considerable energy doing so. It may very well be that passion is the ingredient without which an organization is dying but just doesn't know it yet!

EI COMPETENCIES AND LEADERSHIP

Prior to 1973, the conventional wisdom was that if you wanted to select the right person for a job, you should find those who had high IQ, technical skills, or personality. David McClelland proposed a truly radical alternative. He proposed that an organization first study employees who were already outstanding performers in a given position, then compare them with those employees who were just average at it. This approach yields not just the threshold abilities for a position—those basic skills that everyone must have to do the job—but most importantly, the *distinguishing* competencies. Once these are known, suggested McClelland, you can either choose individuals who already possess the required competencies or develop them. This practice is now standard in world-class organizations that have developed a leadership competency model to identify, train, and promote likely stars.

An example of such a leadership competence model is one developed by a division of Siemens under the guidance of Lyle Spencer. They identified a pool of star leaders, whose growth in revenues and return on sales placed their performance in the top 10 to 15 percent. These branch managers had annual sales that were 75 percent higher than those of the average managers: nearly 30 million dollars, compared to 17 million, and a 106 percent higher return on sales (Spencer, 2001).

When the stars were compared with the managers whose performance was only average, four EI competencies—but not a single technical or purely cognitive competency—emerged as the unique strengths of the stars. These were the drive to achieve results, the ability to take initiative, skills in collaboration and teamwork, and the ability to lead teams (Goleman, et al, 2002, p. 36).

EI

*There are four components
to EI:*

- *self-awareness*
- *self-management*
- *social awareness*
- *relationship
  management*

The conclusion, then, is that emotional intelligence is a greater determinant of leader success than purely cognitive skills or technical ability. Furthermore, the good news is that these are not genetically based but can be learned, so that any individual can potentially improve his or her leadership skills.

Just what, however, is meant by emotional intelligence? And can it be developed, or is it genetic?

EMOTIONAL INTELLIGENCE IN DEPTH

There are four major components to EI: self-awareness, self-management, social awareness, and relationship management. Each of these, in turn, consists of a number of subcomponents.

Self-Awareness

❑ *Emotional self-awareness.* Leaders who have high emotional self-awareness are in tune with their inner emotions and understand how their feelings affect their job performance. They are aware of their guiding values

161

and are candid and authentic, able to speak openly about their emotions or with conviction about their guiding vision.

❑ *Accurate self-assessment.* Leaders need to know their strengths and limitations. These individuals usually have a sense of humor about themselves and welcome constructive feedback.

❑ *Self-confidence.* When they have an accurate assessment of their abilities, leaders can play to their strengths. They often have a presence that makes them stand out in a group.

Self-Management

❑ *Self-control.* Leaders with emotional self-control manage their disturbing emotions, even channeling them in useful ways. This is exemplified by the leader who stays calm and clear-headed during a crisis or high-stress situation. This was the hallmark of Churchill and Giuliani during their trying situations.

❑ *Transparency.* Leaders who are transparent live their values. They are open and candid with others about their feelings, beliefs, and actions. They readily admit their mistakes or faults and confront unethical behavior in others.

❑ *Adaptability.* Such leaders are able to juggle multiple demands without losing focus or energy, and are able to "roll with the punches."

❑ *Achievement.* Leaders with this strength have high personal standards that drive them to continually seek ways to improve—both for themselves and their followers. They are constantly learning and teaching others ways to do things better.

❑ *Initiative.* Individuals who have this quality don't wait to be told. They take control and cut through red tape when they see an opportunity.

❑ *Optimism.* Leaders with optimism are characterized by seeing the glass as "half-full" instead of "half-empty." Their optimism is genuine, however, and they tend to see others positively, expecting the best of them.

Social Awareness

❑ *Empathy.* Empathic leaders are able to sense a wide range of emotional signals in an individual or group. They are able to get along well with people of diverse backgrounds or cultures. And they are able to respond to the signals they pick up in ways that let people know they really understand them.

❑ *Organizational awareness.* Leaders with high social awareness are able to read the political climate of the organization, to detect critical social networks, and to read key power relationships.

❑ *Service.* Individuals with this competence are service-minded and monitor customer satisfaction to ensure that customers are getting what they need.

Relationship Management

❑ *Inspiration.* Leaders who can inspire others with a compelling vision tend to "walk the talk," and offer a sense of common purpose beyond the day-to-day tasks, thus making work exciting.

❑ *Influence.* Leaders adept in influence are persuasive and engaging when they address a group. They are able to find just the right appeal for a given listener as well, and build support for their initiatives.

❑ *Developing others.* This is the central trait of the natural coach. They show a genuine interest in those they are helping, understanding their goals, strengths, and weaknesses.

❑ *Change catalyst.* Leaders who act as catalysts recognize when change is needed. They challenge the status quo and act as champions for a new order. You will remember that this was one of the practices discovered by Kouzes and Posner in their research on leadership.

❑ *Conflict management.* The difference between conflict management and conflict resolution is that one manages conflict by actually drawing out different perspectives while preventing such differences from becoming interpersonal and divisive. In conflict resolution, you listen to differences that exist, and then you help the parties reach common ground and develop a mutually acceptable solution. Good leaders need to be able to do both.

❑ *Teamwork and collaboration.* Leaders who are good team players are able to draw others into active, enthusiastic commitment to a collective effort. They spend time developing and cementing close relationships beyond mere work obligations.

As you can see, 18 subcomponents combine to make up EI. Does this mean that an effective leader will be equally proficient at all of them? Hardly. No individual is likely to be that broadly competent. However, Goleman argues that they must have some degree of skill in many of them, and empathy tends to be very high on the list of competencies that one needs. The "clueless" leader is unlikely to build close relationships, inspire a compelling vision, or understand his or her impact on others.

LEADERSHIP STYLES—AGAIN!

There seem to be more leadership styles than there are people who write on the topic, and that is a lot! However, on close scrutiny, you begin to see that there is considerable overlap, which there should be if the research is valid. It is just that each author chooses different labels to convey his or her idea of the research findings.

Goleman and his partners have identified six styles of leadership that have clear relationships to others that you have seen earlier in this book. Before introducing them, I should mention that

Goleman has said that effective leaders create *resonance* with their followers, whereas those who are ineffective create *dissonance*. Obviously, resonance is a state in which people are energized by a leader, while dissonance would be the opposite.

Four of Goleman's styles create the kind of resonance that boosts performance. These are visionary, coaching, affiliative, and democratic. Two other styles can be useful, but if the leader is not careful, they create dissonance. These are pacesetting and commanding.

Again, these conclusions are based on a study of 3,871 executives. "Results showed that, all other things being equal, leaders who used styles with a positive emotional impact saw decidedly better financial returns than those who did not" (Goleman, et al, 2002, p. 54). In addition, the findings showed that effective leaders practiced several of these styles, rather than just a single one. In fact, the style chosen depended on the situation.

The Visionary Leader

The visionary leader moves people toward shared dreams. This is, in fact, what many of us think of when we think of true leadership—the individual who inspires us to pursue some lofty future outcome. It is Mulally's compelling vision—the 777 that goes from "Denver to Honolulu on a hot day." It is Martin Luther King's "I Have a Dream" speech, which may be one of the most famous delivered in the 20th century. The visionary leader has the most strongly positive effect on the climate of an organization. This style is most appropriate when a clear direction is needed or when changes in the environment require a company to develop a new vision.

Goleman and his colleagues caution that the style doesn't work in every situation, however. It fails when a leader is working with a team of experts who are more experienced than he. In such a situation, a leader who expounds a grand vision may be viewed as pompous or simply out of step with the agenda.

Nevertheless, the visionary approach should be used more often than not.

The Coaching Style

Although most people believe that every leader should be a good coach, leaders actually tend to adopt this approach least often. The excuse is that they simply don't have time to work one-on-one with followers. In failing to adopt this style, however, they miss a great opportunity.

Coaching conveys a genuine interest in people, as opposed to just seeing them as tools. It generates a very positive climate, and ultimately affects the *bottom line* positively, even though its thrust is on personal development.

The coaching style succeeds in part by helping individuals identify their strengths and weaknesses, and then tying those to their personal and career aspirations. This ultimately causes employees to gravitate toward the aspects of the job that they like most, which keeps them motivated, which, in turn, yields high performance. As a part of this, coaches are good at delegating— giving employees challenging assignments that stretch them, rather than tasks that simply get the job done.

Coaching doesn't work with all employees, of course. It works best with those who show initiative and want more professional development. It will fail with those who lack motivation or who need excessive hand-holding, or when the leader does not have the expertise needed to help the person along. When executed poorly, it smacks of micro-managing, which many employees resent.

The Affiliative Style: Relationship Building

Leaders who practice the affiliative style tend to value people and their feelings. They place less emphasis on goals and tasks and more on employees' emotional needs. This style is limited as a driver of performance, but it has a very positive impact on a group's climate, which indirectly pushes performance upward. Most importantly, affiliative leaders build extremely high loyalty to the organization. This means that they are likely to retain talent even when other organizations may be losing it.

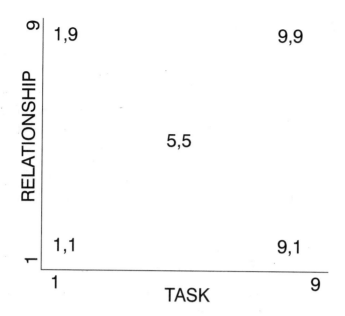

Figure 12.1.
The Blake and Mouton Grid®.

This style is the one to use when you need to build team cohesiveness, increase morale, improve communication, or repair broken trust in an organization. It is also an important style to use when dealing with Asian or Latin American individuals or groups, for whom building strong relationships is a prerequisite for doing business.

The caveat here is that the affiliative style cannot be the only style a leader adopts or nothing will get done. This is the "country club" style discussed by Robert Blake and Jane Mouton in their book, *Managerial Grid* (1964). In this book, they map several styles of leadership on a grid that indicates a manager's concern for task and concern for relationship with followers, with the axes being graduated from 1 to 9 points. A 9-9 style is high concern for task and high concern for relationship, which Blake and Mouton suggested is optimal for a leader (see Figure 12.1). A 1-9 style would be low concern for task and high concern for relationships, which is the country club style. As they suggested, a group run exclusively in this manner will report very high degrees of satisfaction with relationships but probably won't get much done.

The Democratic Style

This style works best when the leader is unsure what direction to take and needs input from competent employees. However, if such input never results in any kind of action, the democratic style backfires. Notice also that you seek the advice of employees when they are informed and competent. The democratic style *is not* appropriate in times of crisis, when the situation demands immediate decisions.

Pacesetting: Use Sparingly

This style is more likely to create dissonance than resonance, so it should be used with caution. Still, there are times that call for it. During the entrepreneurial phase of a company's life, it is appropriate. It also works for a group when members are highly motivated, competent, and need little direction. Pacesetting is very goal directed, driving employees to achieve high levels of performance. However, it may be the 1 to 9 style of Blake and Mouton's grid, in which the only concern of the leader is for task and there is little or no concern for relationships.

A pacesetting leader may push so hard for results that employees are left feeling like pawns, resulting in dissonance. More often than not, pacesetting creates a bad work climate. While moderate pressure to achieve a deadline (for instance) can motivate, too much pressure may be debilitating. People lose sight of vision—which is energizing—and focus only on survival. At best, pacesetting should be a short-term style, used during crisis or situations that need a quick spurt of energy.

The Command Style

Commonly called the command-and-control style, once employed by the military, this style is seldom appropriate. The disaster situation is one time when it works. But even then it comes up short. Giuliani may have adopted some command-and-control stances following the September 11 attacks, but he took time to address the emotional concerns of people as well. He expressed his own sorrow and empathized with the American public. In doing so, his command-and-control approach most likely was seen as appropriate: Here was a man who was taking charge, supporting the search-and-rescue effort, directing resources to those places where they were needed.

In its extreme form, the command style becomes the SOB style. There are many accounts of leaders who have been highly effective using this style. However, when the peripheral effects of this style are examined, the command style usually comes up lacking. The turnaround CEO often adopts this style, and while such individuals may improve bottom-line results, the net result is to destroy the organization in many cases.

One such CEO turned around a hospital by laying off a percentage of the nursing staff, a move that cut costs and naturally improved the bottom line. However, it also reduced the capability of the hospital to give the required care to patients, leading to increased complaints from them. This also led to a loss of clients as people needing medical care went to a competitor. Ultimately, the CEO had to hire back most of the nurses he had dismissed, but he never understood that his style was the cause of the problem.

FLEXIBILITY—AGAIN

A central theme of the situational leadership model of Hersey and Blanchard is that a leader must have the flexibility to adopt any of the four styles (directing, consulting, participative, delegative) as the situation demands it. Goleman and his colleagues have found the same thing in reference to their six styles. "The more of the six styles a leader can deploy . . . the better. Leaders who have mastered four or more, our data suggest—especially the resonance-building styles—foster the very best climate and business performance (Goleman, et al, 2002, p. 85).

EMOTIONAL INTELLIGENCE AND THE HBDI

You will remember that the HBDI measures one's preference for thinking in certain ways, and that the C quadrant deals with thinking emotionally and interpersonally. Having a low score in this quadrant would suggest that a person has little preference for thinking about such issues. This would imply that the person may not show a high degree of empathy for others, may not spend much time building relationships, and might therefore show signs of low emotional intelligence in these areas.

What is important to remember, though, is that the measure is of preference, not ability. Through practice, a person can develop thinking skills in each of the four quadrants, and this is definitely in line with Goleman's claim that leaders can increase their EI. In fact, he says that most of us improve with age, though that does not always follow.

So, if you happen to score low in this quadrant, don't shoot yourself. Just put together a self-development plan to build your ability in the C quadrant.

I also believe that a high score in the D quadrant would suggest that you tend to be visionary, which is the most important and powerful of the resonance-building styles. However, if you have a high D-quadrant score and a low C-quadrant score, it may suggest that you are not able to sell your vision to your followers, due to a lack of empathy with them. Nevertheless, you can again compensate if you understand the area that must be addressed.

13

Credibility and Trust

*N*o *one will follow* a person who is not trusted, and to be trusted, the leader must be credible in the eyes of a follower. When the designated leader lacks credibility, people may turn for guidance to someone else in the group whom they trust and respect. This means that the official leader may not be able to actually lead the team at all. To sum up, the leader must be viewed as having the right to lead, the qualifications to lead, and to be going in a direction that followers want to go in themselves.

You may think that one's position in the organization would be enough, but it is not. I have discussed the different kinds of power in Chapter 11. Position power is the power granted to an individual by the organization. Such power gives a manager the right to exercise sanctions over employees and to reward them monetarily (if the position is that of a department manager, for example), but

CREDIBILITY & TRUST

*No one will
follow a
person who
is not
trusted.*

it does not confer status on the individual leader. Leadership is only granted by followers.

COMPONENTS OF CREDIBILITY

Many years ago, a young woman who had just graduated from college attended my seminar on project management. Shortly afterward, she was given a project to manage for which most of her team were located in another city, about 800 miles away. The team members were mostly very senior engineers, and she knew almost immediately that she had a problem. She had two strikes against her. She was young. And she was a woman. In addition, the distance presented a major obstacle because she was not present most of the time and was therefore not visible as a leader.

It was very clear to her that these older, more experienced engineers resented her, even though she herself was an engineer and a very competent one at that. So she told me that she made it very clear to them that she was not there to guide them technically. She was there to help them get the resources they needed to do their jobs. She would guide them in achieving the project mission, and she would buffer them from outside influences as best she could. In addition, she made a monthly trip to visit them, just to talk, ask questions, and show them support. It took some time, but eventually they accepted her and even respected her.

I am sure that, if we could have asked the team members about their concerns, there would have been several:

- ❑ Does she know what she is doing—especially in terms of our work? Does she understand the technical issues we face?
- ❑ How is she going to treat us? Is she going to direct us technically?
- ❑ She's just out of school. How can she possibly have the right to lead us? We're far more experienced. Why didn't the company pick one of us to lead this project?
- ❑ Does she even appreciate our expertise?
- ❑ Can she provide us with any rewards?

I also believe that these questions are on the minds of many people in project teams, unless they already know the project leader from previous experience. For that reason, a project leader has to address these concerns if he or she is to achieve a true leadership role with the team.

TECHNICAL TEAMS AND CREDIBILITY

I believe that leaders of technical teams face an especially hard time with credibility. In my experience, engineers and programmers tend to not respect leaders who lack technical skills, and believe that only another engineer or programmer should be the project leader. You will remember that I said in Chapter 1 that perceived differences make relationship-building difficult, while perceived similarities work to build relationships. So technical people sometimes think that if you are not "one of them," you can't understand their needs, you can't fully support them, and you won't be able to appreciate their contributions (which, remember, is an essential behavior for an effective leader). And there is some truth in this.

In fact, I recently met an individual who is heading a group of Information systems people, and credibility with them has been almost impossible for him to develop because he has an undergraduate degree in physics and a master's in a liberal arts discipline. His technical undergraduate degree carries a small amount of weight with his group, but not much. Furthermore, he fired their beloved leader—who had a programming background—a move that certainly has won him no points with them.

It may be that he can position himself as the keeper of the vision, supplier of resources, and champion for their work, and thereby win them over, but he definitely can't do it based on technical expertise.

TRUST

Trust is another factor that requires that people see you as either similar to them or as understanding their needs and being willing to help them meet those needs. They must see a person as having integrity, as being honest, and as not being out to "get them." The person who is totally narcissistic, who only cares about achieving his own objectives, will be seen as untrustworthy. The person who lies, manipulates, who feigns interest in others while trying to simply further his own objectives will not be trusted.

Trust can take a long time to build and can be destroyed in a split second. Playing back-stabbing politics, for example, causes others to distrust a person who engages in this practice. They figure that they will be next, if they get in the way of the back-stabber.

Knowing that another person has cheated someone else, has committed a crime, or has questionable character leads to distrust. I have heard that "there is honor among thieves," meaning that a thief may steal from others but not a fellow thief. I just wonder if there is any thief who really believes that a "colleague" can be trusted.

EMOTIONAL INTELLIGENCE, CREDIBILITY, AND TRUST

One of the self-management components is transparency, which is an authentic openness to others about one's feelings, beliefs, and actions. Transparency allows a leader to be seen as having integrity, which means she can be trusted. Integrity keeps a person from acting on impulse—something she might later regret. It also means a leader lives her values; in the eyes of followers, she "walks the talk." One of the quickest ways for a leader to lose credibility is to say one thing and do another.

Relationship management is very important to a leader's credibility. Managing relationships boils down to handling other people's emotions. This requires that leaders be aware of their own emotions and have empathy for their followers. If a leader behaves manipulatively or feigns interest in people, they will sense this falseness and distrust the leader. This means that managing relationships successfully requires authenticity—acting from one's genuine feelings.

As I stated in Chapter 12, coaching is also a style that helps build trust in followers. By showing a personal interest in them, expressing a desire to help them further their own goals and career aspirations, a leader can gain trust and credibility. It may well be that the leader of the IS group mentioned above could gain trust through more one-on-one meetings with his followers, even though he is in no position to coach them technically. He is, however, able to coach them around career development, and this itself may be enough.

BUILDING CREDIBILITY

Every time I teach a seminar, my first task is to build credibility with my group. Recently I taught for a group that bordered on being openly hostile. When I got up in front of them and said, "Good morning," not a single person replied. I believe it was the first time in my 20 years of teaching that this has happened. Needless to say, I thought I was in for a horrible three days.

So I started talking about the course and what we were going to do. I told them that there would be parts of it that some would say they would never use, and that for me, the goal was for them to find those parts that they could use. I also told them that seeing how to apply the methods in their own projects might be hard, and I promised to help in whatever way I could.

Then I told them about my background as an engineer (since these were technical people, that mattered). I told them that I had managed projects by the seat of the pants for about 10 years before receiving any formal training in the discipline, and that I could vouch for the improvement to be gained through a better approach.

I told them some survey data about the percentage of projects in their discipline that fail because of poor project management, showed how much those failures cost, and told them that with a small improvement they could get big gains. I shared several specific examples, using stories to capture their interest.

Then I asked them to introduce themselves. I asked that they tell me who they were, the job they did, and what objective they had for the class. "If you were sentenced to be here," I said, "you still may as well try to get something from the class." My line about being sentenced almost always gets a laugh—and it did, even from this group. It lets them know that I understand the reality of their situation, but that I am willing to have a little fun with it.

In fact, I set the stage for them to have some fun. As they introduced themselves, they referred to themselves as prisoners, but said that they could use some help. A few said they were willing prisoners. Overall, everyone had a laugh about the situation.

The laughter alone helped. Goleman and his colleagues have said that laughter is contagious. It offers a uniquely trustworthy sign of friendliness. So if you can get a group laughing early on, you can often win them over.

I next asked them to talk about their projects. I asked what was working and what was not. As they told me about these aspects of their jobs, I offered comments to validate what they were saying.

By the time I started teaching, there was a marked change in the climate of the group, and when I ended on the third day,

Accept NO "stale" workers

———

Offering training and new job opportunities benefits the company and the employee.

people were shaking my hand and telling me how good the program had been. Not everyone was equally satisfied, I'm sure, because you can't win over everyone. But the majority of them were with me.

I believe that several components of emotional intelligence help me do this. One is empathy. I do understand that people are busy and that being required to attend a seminar of questionable merit is an imposition some can hardly afford. Furthermore, there is an implication that if they need to attend this seminar, there is something wrong with them. They are broken in some way, and the boss intends to fix them. I even play on that with them and have some fun with it.

Overall, I try to frame the class as something that is going to make their lives better. I state my role as one of supporting them and helping them. I position the experience in as positive a light as is possible and go on from there. Like Jaime Escalante did with his students, I try to address their needs and show how we will meet them. All of this helps me win over a group that is less than enthusiastic about being there.

One interesting aspect of credibility for me is that my engineering background gives me credibility with technical people when I am talking about psychological factors. I am sure that, if I only had a degree in psychology, they would see me as a touchy-feely "shrink," and would be unconvinced about the validity of what I am saying. However, I am "one of them," and I paid my dues "in the trenches," so they believe me. I tell them about problems I had dealing with my own followers—problems that they themselves are having, and they know that I know what they are facing. Then when I offer suggestions, they listen.

It is a fascinating subject, and one that a leader ignores to his or her own detriment.

14

Putting It All Together

So you've read it all and are wondering, "Now what?" How do I put all of this in context? Most importantly, how do I learn to be a leader? If all I had to do was pass a written test, that would be hard enough—though I'm sure I could do it—but I actually have to behave in ways that I don't feel comfortable with. What do I do?

My first suggestion is that you recognize how skills are developed. You certainly don't learn them through reading a book. You learn them by practicing them. You also learn by failing.

That itself is a scary thought, but it is true that we learn very little from our successes, and a lot from failure. I know, I hear you. You're saying you can't afford to fail. If you screw up you may get fired or at least penalized on the job. That's why you have to fail in a way that doesn't count toward your job evaluation.

SIMULATORS

Not long ago I got to fly a 767 simulator. It was the most fantastic experience of its kind I have ever had. The experience is so real you forget that you are in a simulator. Everything inside is an exact duplicate of a real airplane. But what is so impressive is that everything you see outside the windows is also absolutely real. And everything you hear sounds like the real thing—the sound of the engines, warnings about traffic ahead, alarms going off telling you you're doing something wrong in flying the plane, such as banking too sharply, and so on. I can understand after this experience how a person learns to fly a plane without getting into a real one—then actually gets into a real plane and actually pilots it.

Of course the real beauty of the simulator is that you can "crash" without killing yourself and destroying a multi-million dollar airplane. I landed the simulator several times (with considerable help from my instructor co-pilot, I should say) without crashing, although I hit hard on my third landing and felt the plane bounce up, which I have experienced several times in real landings. But I will bet you that if there had been more time and the instructor had handed off more work for me to do, I would have become overloaded with the complexity of it all and crashed. And still "walked away."

So you have to find a way to crash without getting hurt. You have to be able to fail without having it count against you. And the best way to do this is through simulation. You play-act various scenarios. You try out the behaviors described in this book. You get comfortable with them. Then when the time comes to actually engage in them back on the job, you will find them easy.

I was telling a pilot about my simulator experience, and he said that the real airplane is actually easier to fly than the simulator. He said the actual airplane is more responsive than the simulator. I don't know if this is a deliberate design element, though I suspect that it is. I know that athletes practice more strenuously than they think they will have to play in competition, so that the "real event" seems easier. Michael Flatley, the Irish dancer, practices with shoes containing weights, so that when he goes on stage in front of an audience, his feet feel lighter and more nimble.

So practice some really difficult situations. Have someone else play the other parts in the situation and make your life difficult. Then the real event will be a breeze.

This is the way children learn to play adult roles. As we get older, we quit play-acting, but it is the most effective way to learn behavioral skills that you will ever find. If you don't like the term *role- playing,* call it skill practice, because that's what it is.

You may remember that one of the EI components is to be able to control your emotions. During my training in neurolinguistic programming, John Grinder suggested that we learn to appear outwardly angry while we were inwardly calm, and vice versa— to appear outwardly calm when we were actually angry. I can do the first one pretty well, though I confess I have more trouble appearing calm when I'm angry. My face gives me away most of the time. This may be in part because it is hard to make oneself angry so that appearing calm can be practiced.

MENTAL REHEARSAL

You also gain tremendously from mental rehearsal. Just sit down and imagine a scenario and how you will behave in it. Go through it a number of times. Imagine variations, so that you develop flexibility. Try to imagine what you would see, hear, taste, touch, and smell in the actual situation. This engages all five senses.

Studies have found that mental rehearsal can be almost as effective as physical rehearsal—even for such things as sports and playing musical instruments. (I'm sure if any children get their hands on this book there is going to be a lot of mental practice of their instruments and not much of the real thing!)

I have found myself doing this when I am faced with an unpleasant situation—such as having to council or terminate an employee. It helps a lot. I also read a book by Larry Wilson, who founded Wilson Learning Systems, and was the youngest person ever to be inducted into the Million Dollar Club for insurance salesmen. He was 23 years old when he sold his first million dollars of insurance in a single year. The club officials were so impressed that they asked him to give a speech to the annual convention. The audience would consist of several hundred, and it would be the first speech he had ever had to give to an audience that large.

He was terrified. He found himself imagining a disaster in which he got on the stage and fell flat on his face.

Then it struck him: that was exactly what would happen if he kept imagining failure.

So he turned it around. Every day he spent time visualizing success. He imagined giving his speech to an audience of interested, friendly people who were eager to learn how he had been so successful. After all, that was why he had been asked to speak in the first place, so why not? He imagined that people from the audience would come to the stage to congratulate him.

Finally the big day arrived. He gave his speech.

And it was almost deja vu! People actually did come to the stage to compliment and congratulate him. He was comfortable while giving the speech and noted that the audience was paying rapt attention.

This experience formed a core component of how he later trained salespeople. They had to visualize, to imagine selling successfully. And it will work for you too.

FIND A ROLE MODEL

One of the things children do to learn skills is imitate others. In fact, this is how athletes and musicians learn their skills also. Modeling mastery and excellence helps one develop one's talent. Very little can be learned about excellence by studying pathology.

So find someone who already has a skill that you want to develop and imitate that person. Do be careful about one thing. Some components of skill can be gender specific, so if you are a woman and you imitate a male role model, you may come across as too "masculine" in your own performance, and vice versa.

FIND A COACH

As you practice your learning, you need feedback. You need a person who can help you overcome your problem areas. Videotape may give you good visual and auditory feedback, so that you know where you should focus, but you may not always have a good idea what to do to correct for any difficulties you are having. A coach can help.

A coach must be able to give helpful, constructive feedback to be effective, so select someone who will do so, and if you find that your coach is only giving you negative feedback without giving you help, find another coach.

ENJOY THE JOURNEY

You may remember that one of Mulally's principles is "Enjoy the journey and each other." I enthusiastically recommend this principle to you as you pursue your career as a leader. Have fun. Don't take *yourself* too seriously, but take your goal very seriously. Remember, laughter is the best medicine, and the more fun you can have with your learning the more effective it is likely to be. Really!

Resources for Managers

*F*ollowing is a list of sources of information, books, and professional associations that may be helpful in managing.

CRM Learning: A good source of films for training, including *Mining Group Gold, The Abilene Paradox,* and many others. 2215 Faraday Avenue, Carlsbad, CA 92008. Tel. (800) 421-0833.

Jossey-Bass/Pfeiffer: A source of training programs, training materials, instruments, and books on management. 350 Sansome Street, 5th Floor, San Francisco, CA 94104. Tel. (800) 274-4434. FAX: (800) 569-0443. www.pfeiffer.com

The Lewis Institute, Inc.: Founded by the author, the Institute provides training in project management, team building, and related courses. The core program is Project Management: Tools, Principles, Practices, and has been attended by over 20,000 managers worldwide. 302 Chestnut Mountain Dr., Vinton, VA 24179. Tel. (540) 345-7850. FAX: (540) 345-7844. e-mail: jlewis@lewisinstitute.com. www.lewisinstitute.com

McGraw-Hill Books: Source for other titles on project management. www.mcgraw-hill.com

MindWare: The store for the other 90 percent of your brain. A source of tools, books and other materials for helping enhance learning and creativity in organizations. They have a nice catalog listing their materials. 121 Fifth Ave. NW, New Brighton, MN 55112. Tel. (800) 999-0398. www.mindwareonline.com

Morasco, Vincent: A newspaper clipping service that operates on a pay-per-use basis. You pay only for the clippings you actually make use of. A good source of up-to-the-minute information. Vincent Morasco, 3 Cedar Street, Batavia, NY 14020. Tel. (716) 343-2544.

PBS Home Video: Source of the video *21ˢᵗ Century Jet.* (800) 645-4727. www.shopPBS.com.

Pegasus Communications: Publishers of *The Systems Thinker,* a monthly newsletter. They also have videos by Russell Ackoff and Peter Senge, among others. P.O. Box 943, Oxford, OH 45056-0943. Tel. (800) 636-3796. FAX: (905) 764-7983

Pimsleur International: The most effective way to learn a language on your own is with the cassettes using a method developed by Dr. Paul Pimsleur. Learning is virtually painless. 30 Monument Square, Suite 135, Concord, MA 01742. Tel. (800) 222-5860. FAX: (508) 371-2935.

Project Management Institute: The professional association for project managers. Over 25,000 members nationwide as of July 1997. They have local chapters in most major U.S. cities and a number of countries. 130 S. State Road, Upper Darby, PA 19082. Tel. (610) 734-3330. FAX: (610) 734-3266.

Project Manager Today: This monthly magazine is published in England and has some good articles for the practicing PM. P. O. Box 55, Wockingham, Berkshire, RG40 4ZZ, England. Tel. (44) (0)118 976 1339. FAX (44) (0) 118 976 1944.

Video Arts: A source for management training videos. Originally founded by John Cleese, many of them take a humorous approach to the subjects they cover. 8614 W. Catalpa Ave., Chicago, IL 60656. Tel. (800) 553-0091.

Web sites of interest:

www.joelbarker.com: Joel Barker's Web site
www.interact.com: Russell Ackoff's Web site
www.boeing.com: Boeing's Web site
The Emotional Intelligence Web site

References and Reading List

Ackoff, Russell. *Ackoff's Fables: Irreverent Reflections on Business and Bureaucracy*. New York: Wiley, 1991.

———. *The Art of Problem Solving*. New York: Wiley, 1978.

———. *Creating the Corporate Future*. New York: Wiley, 1981.

———. *The Democratic Corporation*. New York: Oxford University Press, 1994.

Adams, James L. *Conceptual Blockbusting: A Guide to Better Ideas*. 2d ed. New York: W. W. Norton, 1979.

Adams, John D., ed. *Transforming Leadership: From Vision to Results*. Alexandria, VA: Miles River Press, 1986.

Ailes, Roger. *You Are the Message: Secrets of the Master Communicators*. Homewood, IL: Dow Jones-Irwin, 1988.

Albrecht, Karl. *The Northbound Train*. New York: AMACOM, 1994.

Archibald, R. D., and R. L. Villoria. *Network-Based Management Systems (Pert/cpm)*. New York: Wiley, 1967.

Argyris, Chris. *Overcoming Organizational Defenses: Facilitating Organizational Learning*. Boston: Allyn and Bacon, 1990.

Axelrod, Robert. *The Evolution of Cooperation*. New York: Basic Books, 1984.

Barker, Joel A. *Future Edge*. New York: William Morrow, 1992.

———. *Wealth, Innovation & Diversity*. Videotape. Carlsbad, CA: CRM Learning, 2000.

Bauer, Eugene E. *Boeing: The First Century*. Enumclaw, Washington: TABA Publishing, 2000.

Bedi, Hari. *Understanding the Asian Manager*. Singapore: Heinemann Asia, 1992.

Beer, Stafford. *Brain of the Firm.* 2d ed. New York: Wiley, 1981.

Bennis, Warren G. *Managing the Dream: Reflections on Leadership and Change.* Cambridge, MA: Perseus, 2000.

Bennis, Warren G., and Burt Nanus. *Leaders: the Strategies for Taking Charge.* New York: Harper & Row, 1985.

Benveniste, Guy. *Mastering the Politics of Planning.* San Francisco: Jossey-Bass, 1989.

Barnhart, Robert K. *The Barnhart Concise Dictionary of Etymology: The Origins of American English Words.* New York: Harper Collins, 1995.

Blanchard, Benjamin S. *Engineering Organization and Management.* Englewood Cliffs, NJ: Prentice-Hall, 1976.

Blake, Robert, and Jane Mouton. *The Managerial Grid.* Houston: Gulf Publishing, 1964.

Block, Peter. *The Empowered Manager.* 2d ed. San Francisco: Jossey-Bass, 2000.

Bodanis, David. *E=mc²: A Biography of the World's Most Famous Equation.* New York: Walker & Company, 2000.

Brooks, F. P. *The Mythical Man-Month: Essays on Software Engineering.* Reading, MA: Addison-Wesley, 1975.

Bunker, Barbara Benedict, and Billie T. Alban. *Large Group Interventions: Engaging the Whole System for Rapid Change.* San Francisco: Jossey-Bass, 1997.

Burns, James McGregor. *Leadership.* New York: Harper & Row, 1978.

Buzan, Tony. *The Mind Map Book.* New York: NAL/Dutton, 1996.

Carlzon, Jan. *Moments of Truth.* New York: Perennial, 1987.

Cialdini, Robert B. *Influence: The Power of Persuasion.* Rev. ed. . New York: Quill, 1993.

Cleland, David I., and William R. King, eds. *Project Management Handbook.* New York: Van Nostrand Reinhold, 1983.

Cousins, Norman. *Head First: The Biology of Hope and the Healing Power of the Human Spirit.* New York: Penguin Books, 1989.

Covey, Stephen. *The 7 Habits of Highly Effective People.* New York: Fireside Books, 1989.

de Bono, Edward. *New Think.* New York: Avon Books, 1971.

———. *Serious Creativity.* New York: Harper, 1992.

———. *Six Thinking Hats.* Boston: Little, Brown & Co., 1985.

Deming, Edwards. *Out of the Crisis*. Cambridge, MA: Massachusetts Institute of Technology, 1986.

Dimancescu, Dan. *The Seamless Enterprise. Making Cross-Functional Management Work*. New York: Harper, 1992.

Downs, Alan. *Corporate Executions: The Ugly Truth About Layoffs—How Corporate Greed Is Shattering Lives, Companies, and Communities*. New York: AMACOM, 1995.

Drucker, Peter F. *Management: Tasks, Responsibilities, Practices*. New York: Harper & Row, 1973, 1974.

Dyer, Wayne. *You'll See It When You Believe It*. New York: Avon Books, 1989.

Eisenstein, Paul A. "How Toyota's Kentucky Operations Mix People, Processes to Be Best." *Investor's Business Daily* (December 4, 2000)

Fleming, Q. W. *Cost/Schedule Control Systems Criteria*. Chicago: Probus, 1988.

Fleming, Quentin W., and Joel M. Koppelman. *Earned Value Project Management*. Upper Darby, PA: Project Management Institute, 1996.

Fortune, Joyce, and Geoff Peters. *Learning from Failure: The Systems Approach*. Chichester, England: Wiley, 1998.

Frame, J. Davidson. *Managing Projects in Organizations*. San Francisco: Jossey-Bass, 1995.

Frankl, Viktor. *Man's Search for Meaning*. 3d ed. New York: Touchstone, 1984.

Freiberg, Kevin, and Jackie Freiberg. *Nuts! Southwest Airlines' Crazy Recipe for Business and Personal Success*. New York: Broadway Books, 1996.

Gardner, Howard. *Frames of Mind: The Theory of Multiple Intelligences*. New York: Basic Books, 1993.

Garten, Jeffrey E. *The Mind of the C. E. O.* New York: Basic Books, 2001.

Goldratt, Eliyahu M. *Critical Chain*. Great Barrington, MA: The North River Press, 1997.

Goleman, Daniel, Boyatzis, Richard, and McKee, Annie. *Primal Leadership: Realizing the Power of Emotional Intelligence*. Boston: Harvard Business School Press, 2002.

Graham, Robert J., and Randall L. Englund. *Creating an Environment for Successful Projects*. San Francisco: Jossey-Bass, 1997.

Hammer, Michael, and James Champy. *Reengineering the Corporation*. New York: Harper Business, 1993.

Hancock, Graham. *Fingerprints of the Gods.* New York: Crown, 1995.

Harry, Mikel, and Richard Schroeder. *Six Sigma: The Breakthrough Management Strategy Revolutionizing the World's Top Corporations.* New York: Currency, 2000.

Harvey, Jerry B. *The Abilene Paradox: and Other Meditations on Management.* San Diego: University Associates, 1988.

Heller, Robert. *Achieving Excellence.* New York: DK Publishing, 1999.

Heller, Robert, and Tim Hindle. *Essential Manager's Manual.* New York: DK Publishing, 1998.

Herrmann, Ned. *The Creative Brain.* Lake Lure, NC: Brain Books, 1995.

———. *The Whole Brain Business Book.* New York: McGraw-Hill, 1996.

Hersey, Paul, and Kenneth Blanchard. *Management of Organizational Behavior: Utilizing Human Resources.* 4th ed. Englewood Cliffs, NJ: Prentice-Hall, 1981.

Hiebeler, Robert, Thomas Kelly, and Charles Ketteman. *Best Practices: Building Your Business with Customer-Focused Solutions.* New York: Simon and Schuster, 1998.

Highsmith, III, James A. *Adaptive Software Development.* New York: Dorset House, 2000.

Ittner, Christopher D., and David F. Larckner. *A Bigger Yardstick for Company Performance.* London: *The Financial Times* (October 16, 2000).

Janis, Irving, and Leon Mann. *Decision Making.* New York: The Free Press, 1977.

Jones, Russel A. *Self-Fulfilling Prophecies.* Hillsdale, NJ: Lawrence Erlbaum, 1977.

Kayser, Tom. *Mining Group Gold.* New York: McGraw-Hill, 1995.

Keane. *Productivity Management: Keane's Project Management Approach for Systems Development.* 2d ed. Boston: Keane Associates, (800) 239-0296.

Keirsey, David. *Please Understand Me II.* Del Mar, CA: Prometheus Nemesis Book Company, 1998.

Kepner, Charles H., and Benjamin B. Tregoe. *The Rational Manager.* Princeton, NJ: Kepner-Tregoe, Inc., 1965.

Kerzner, Harold. *In Search of Excellence in Project Management.* New York: Van Nostrand, 1998.

———. *Project Management: A Systems Approach to Planning, Scheduling, and Controlling.* 5th ed. New York: Van Nostrand, 1995.

Kiemele, Mark J., and Stephen R. Schmidt. *Basic Statistics. Tools for Continuous Improvement.* 3d ed. Colorado Springs: Air Academy Press, 1993.

Knight, James A. *Value-Based Management: Developing a Systematic Approach to Creating Shareholder Value.* New York: McGraw-Hill, 1998.

Knowles, Malcolm. *Self-Directed Learning.* New York: Association Press, 1975.

Koch, Richard. *The 80/20 Principle.* New York: Doubleday, 1998.

Kormanski, Chuck, and Andrew Mozenter. "A New Model of Team Building: A Technology for Today and Tomorrow." In J. S. Pfeiffer, Editor, *The 1987 Annual: Developing Human Resources.* San Francisco: Jossey-Bass, 1987.

Kouzes, James M., and Barry Z. Posner. *The Leadership Challenge: How to Get Extraordinary Things Done in Organizations.* San Francisco: Jossey-Bass, 1987.

Kroeger, Otto, and Janet Thuesen. *Type Talk At Work.* New York: Delacorte Press, 1992.

Kuhn, Thomas. *The Structure of Scientific Revolutions.* Chicago: University of Chicago Press, 1970.

Leider, Richard J. *Life Skills: Taking Charge of Your Personal and Professional Growth.* Paramus, NJ: Prentice Hall, 1994.

———. *The Power of Purpose: Creating Meaning in Your Life and Work.* San Francisco: Berrett Koehler, 1997.

Lerner, Michael. *The Politics of Meaning.* Reading, MA: Addison-Wesley, 1996.

Lewis, James. *Fundamentals of Project Management.* New York: AMACOM, 1993.

———. *Mastering Project Management.* New York: McGraw-Hill, 1998.

———. *The Project Manager's Desk Reference.* 2d ed. New York: McGraw-Hill, 2000.

———. *Team-Based Project Management.* New York: AMACOM, 1997.

MacMillan, Ian C., and Rita Gunther McGrath. *Corporate Ventures: Maximising Gains.* London: *Financial Times* (October 16, 2000).

Maidique, Modesto, and Billie Jo Zirger. *The New Product Learning Cycle.* Research Policy. (Cited in Peters, 1987.)

Maier, Norman R. F. *Psychology in Industry.* Boston: Houghton Mifflin, 1955.

Maloney, Lawrence D. "For the Love of Flying." *Design News* 51, no. 5, (March 4, 1996).

March, James, and Herbert Simon. *Organizations*. New York: Wiley, 1966.

Maslow, Abraham. *Motivation and Personality*. 2d ed. New York: Harper & Row, 1970.

McCartney, Scott. "Out of the Blue. How Two Pacific Nations Became Oceanic Aces of Air-Traffic Control." *The Wall Street Journal* (Friday, December 29, 2000).

McClelland, David. *Power: The Inner Experience*. New York: Halsted Press, 1975.

Michalko, Michael. *Thinkertoys*. Berkeley, CA: Ten Speed Press, 1995.

Miller, William C. *The Creative Edge: Fostering Innovation Where You Work*. Reading, MA: Addison-Wesley, 1986.

Mintzberg, Henry. *Mintzberg on Management*. New York: The Free Press, 1989.

Moder, Joseph J., Cecil R. Phillips, and Edward W. Davis. *Project Management with Cpm, Pert, and Precedence Diagraming*. 3d ed. New York: Van Nostrand, 1983.

Morrison, Terri, Wayne Conaway, and George Borden. *Kiss, Bow, or Shake Hands*. Holbrook, MA: Adams Media Corporation, 1994.

Mouzelis, N. P. "Bureaucracy," *The New Encyclopedia Britannica*. 15th ed., Macropaedia 3 (1974).

Nadler, Gerald, and Shozo Hibino. *Breakthrough Thinking*. Rocklin, CA: Prima Publishing, 1990.

Nellore, Rajesh. "R&D Structures to Keep the Focus on Products." London: *Financial Times* (December 11, 2000).

von Oech, Roger. *A Whack on the Side of the Head*. New York: Warner, 1983.

———. *A Kick in the Seat of the Pants*. New York: Warner, 1986.

Packard, Vance. *The Pyramid Climbers*. New York: McGraw-Hill, 1962.

Pasmore, William. *Designing Effective Organizations: The Sociotechnical Systems Perspective*. New York: Wiley, 1988.

Patterson, Marvin. *Accelerating Innovation: Improving the Processes of Product Development*. New York: Van Nostrand Reinhold, 1993.

Peter, Lawrence J. *The Peter Principle*. New York: William Morrow, 1969.

Peters, Tom. *Liberation Management*. New York: Knopf, 1992.

————. *Thriving on Chaos.* New York: Knopf, 1987.

————. The WOW Project. *Fast Company* (May 1999).

Peters, Tom, and Bob Waterman. *In Search of Excellence.* New York: Harper and Row, 1982.

Pinto, Jeffrey K. *Power and Politics in Project Management.* Upper Darby, PA: Project Management Institute, 1996.

Pinto, Jeffrey K., ed. *The Project Management Institute Project Management Handbook.* San Francisco: Jossey-Bass, 1998.

Ray, M., and R. Myers. *Creativity in Business.* Garden City, NY: Doubleday, 1986.

Rickards, Tudor. *Problem Solving through Creative Analysis.* Epping, Essex, England: Gower Press, 1975.

Rosen, Robert H. *Leading People: The 8 Proven Principles for Success in Business.* New York: Penguin Books, 1996.

Rosenthal, R., and L. Jacobson. *Pygmalion in the Classroom.* New York: Holt, Rinehart, and Winston, 1968.

Saaty, Thomas L. *Decision Making for Leaders.* Pittsburgh: RWS Publications, 1995.

Sabbagh, Karl. *Twenty-First Century Jet.* New York: Scribner, 1996.

Schuster, John P., Jill Carpenter, and Patricia Kane. *The Power of Open-Book Management.* New York: Wiley, 1996.

Senge, Peter. *The Fifth Discipline.* New York: Doubleday, 1990.

————. Interview in *Fast Company* (May 1999). Smith, Hyrum W. *The 10 Natural Laws of Successful Time and Life Management.* New York: Warner Books, 1994.

Smith, Preston G., and Reinertsen, Donald G. *Developing Products in Half the Time.* New York: Van Nostrand, 1995.

Spencer, Lyle. "The Economic Value of Emotional Intelligence Competencies and EIC-Based HR Programs," in *The Emotionally Intelligent Workplace.* Cary Cherniss and Daniel Goleman, eds. San Francisco: Jossey-Bass, 2001.

Stacey, Ralph D. *Complexity and Creativity in Organizations.* San Francisco: Berrett-Koehler, 1996.

Steiner, Claude. *Scripts People Live By.* 2d. ed. New York: Grove Weidenfeld, 1990.

Sykes, Charles. *A Nation of Victims: The Decay of the American Character.* New York: St. Martin's Press, 1992.

————. *Dumbing Down Our Kids.* New York: St. Martin's Press, 1995.

Treacy, Michael, and Fred Wiersema. *The Discipline of Market Leaders.* Reading, MA: Addison-Wesley, 1995.

Tuckman, Bruce W. *Development Sequence in Small Groups.* Psychological Bulletin, 1965.

Vroom, Victor, and Arthur Jago. *The New Leadership.* Englewood Cliffs, NJ: 1988.

Vroom, Victor, and Phillip Yetton. *Leadership and Decision Making.* Pittsburgh: University of Pittsburgh Press, 1973.

Walpole, Ronald E. *Introduction to Statistics.* 2d ed. New York: Macmillan, 1974.

Watzlawick, Paul, John Weakland, and Richard Fisch. *Change: Principles of Problem Formulation and Problem Resolution.* New York: Norton, 1974.

Weisbord, Marvin. *Productive Workplaces.* San Francisco: Jossey Bass, 1987.

Weisbord, Marvin, ed. *Discovering Common Ground: How Future Search Conferences Bring People Together to Achieve Breakthrough Innovation, Empowerment, Shared Vision, and Collaborative Action.* San Francisco: Berrett-Koehler, 1992.

Weisbord, Marvin, and Sandra Janoff. *Future Search: An Action Guide to Finding Common Ground in Organizations and Communities.* San Francisco: Berrett-Koehler, 1995.

Wheatley, Margaret. *Leadership and New Science.* San Francisco: Berrett-Koehler, 1992.

White, Gregory L. "In Order to Grow, GM Finds That the Order of the Day Is Cutbacks." *The Wall Street Journal* (Monday, December 18, 2000).

Wing, R. L. *The Tao of Power.* New York: Doubleday, 1986.

Wysocki, Robert K. *Effective Project Management.* 2d ed. New York: Wiley, 2000.

Wysocki, Robert K, and James P. Lewis. *The World-Class Project Manager.* Boston: Perseus Books, 2000.

Young, S. David, and Stephen F. O'Byrne. *EVA® and Value-Based Management.* New York: McGraw-Hill, 2001.

Zander, Rosamund Stone, and Benjamin Zander. *The Art of Possibility.* Boston: Harvard Business School Press, 2000.

Index

Herrmann Brain Dominance Instrument
(HBDI) (*Cont.*):
    scales, 67
    score, 61
Herrmann, Ned, 59, 63, 68
Herrmann, Ned (model), 59–64, 66
Hersey, Paul, 81–82, 169
Herzberg, Frederick, 10
Hidden agendas, 111
Higher-level managers, 150
Hippocrates, 30
Hitler, Adolph, 2
    speech, 118
Hobby, motivation, 51–52
House of Commons, 103
Human beings, nature, 113
Human relations skills, 11
Human resources administrators, 45
Humanities, inclusion, 44
Hunters. *See* Chief hunters

I leaders, contrast. *See* Leaders
Idealist temperament (NF), 32, 36, 42
    characteristics, 43
    individuals, motivation, 44
    interests, 44–45
    project manager, 37
Idealists, 32, 36, 45, 67
Identity, 71
Image. *See* Self-image
Implementation planning, 40
Inclusion. *See* People
    concerns, 88–89
    scores, 89
Indifference, acts, 153
Influence, 120, 133, 163. *See also*
    Interpersonal influence
    methods, categories, 134–140
    process, 15
    relationship. *See* Power; Reciprocity
Information, 140
    deletion/distortion, 111
    meaning, relationship, 120–121
    monetary value, 143
    power, 143
    processing, 122–124
    sharing, 144
Initiative, 162
Innovator. *See* Helper/innovator

Inspiration, 163
Integrity, 145
Intelligence, 50, 83. *See also* Emotional
    intelligence
    assessment, 55
    Keirsey, viewpoint, 37
    kinds, 54
    relationship. *See* Temperaments
    value, 56
Intelligence quotient (IQ), 157, 160
Interest of the temperaments. *See*
    Temperaments
Interests. *See* Artisan; Guardian
    temperament; Idealist temperament;
    Rational temperament
Internal compliance, 138–139
Internal dialog, 124
Internal emotion, 124
Interpersonal approach, 60, 62, 64
Interpersonal influence, 133
Interpersonal issues, 64
Interpersonal skills, gaining, 13
Interpersonal thinking, 64
Interpretation, ability, 29
Interviews, 52
Introversion. *See* Extroversion/introversion
Introverts, 28, 90
Intuition. *See* Sensing/intuition
Involvement. *See* Vision involvement
    persistence
IQ. *See* Intelligence quotient
Iron hand rule, 115
IS group, 175

Jacobson, L., 20, 107
Jefferson, Thomas, 33
Job. *See* Operations-oriented jobs; Routine
    jobs
    commitment, 9
    direction, 99
    dissatisfaction, 158
    interview, 74
    maturity, 87
    motivation, 51
    planning, 99
    position, differences, 58
    requirement, 62
    talent, matching, 78
    satisfaction, 54

About the Author

*J*ames P. Lewis, Ph.D. is an experienced project manager, who now teaches seminars on the subject throughout the United States, England, and the Far East. His solid, no-nonsense approach is largely the result of the 15 years he spent in industry, working as an electrical engineer, engaged in the design and development of communication equipment. He held various positions, including Project Manager, Product Engineering Manager, and Chief Engineer, for Aerotron, Inc., and ITT Telecommunications, both of Raleigh, NC. He also was a Quality Manager for ITT Telecom, managing a department of 63 quality engineers, line inspectors, and test technicians.

While he was an engineering manager, he began working on a doctorate in organizational psychology because of his conviction that a manager can only succeed by developing good interpersonal skills.

From 1980 to 2000, Dr. Lewis trained over 20,000 supervisors and managers in Argentina, Canada, England, Germany, India, Indonesia, Malaysia, Mexico, Singapore, Sweden, Thailand, and the United States and continues to train about 1,000 individuals each year. He has written articles for *Training and Development Journal*, *Apparel Industry* magazine, and *Transportation and Distribution* magazine, and is the author of *Project Planning, Scheduling and*

Control; Mastering Project Management; The Project Manager's Desk Reference; Working Together: 12 Principles for Achieving Excellence in Managing Projects, Teams, and Organizations; Fundamentals of Project Management: Developing Core Competencies to Help Outperform the Competition, and *Team-Based Project Management.* He is co-author, with Bob Wysocki, of *The World-Class Project Manager: A Professional Development Guide.* The first edition of *Project Planning, Scheduling and Control* has been published in a Spanish edition, and the AMACOM book *Fundamentals of Project Management* has been published in Spanish and Portuguese.

He has a B.S. in Electrical Engineering and a Ph.D. in Psychology, both from NC State University in Raleigh. He is a member of several professional societies, including the Project Management Institute and The American Society for Training and Development. He is also a certified Herrmann Brain Dominance Instrument practitioner.

He is president of The Lewis Institute, Inc., a training and consulting company specializing in project management, which he founded in 1981.

Jim is married to the former Lea Ann McDowell, and they live in Vinton, Virginia.